Buddhist Monumental Heritage of sTod Valley in Lahul

Buddhist Monumental Heritage of sTod Valley in Lahul

Chhering Dorje
Tobdan

Kaveri Books
New Delhi - 110002

ISBN : 978-93-86463-21-0
First Published in 2021

Published by
Kaveri Books
4832/24, Ansari Road, Daryaganj,
New Delhi - 110 002 (India)
Ph. : 011-4707 2321
E-mail : info@kaveribooks.com
kaveribooks@gmail.com
Website : www.kaveribooks.com

Typesetting at Creative Graphics, Delhi

PRINTED IN INDIA

Preface

The present monograph is an attempt to document and describe the existing Buddhist monumental heritages in sTod valley of Lahul. These remains have been preserved by the inhabitants of the area for centuries. The first chapter is devoted, in brief, to the advent of Buddhism — Indian and Tibetan-in Lahul while the details on Monastery of Gemur and its subsidiary shrines have been described in the second chapter. The details of other religious structures in sTod vallay have been given in the third chapter. The fourth chapter is entirely devoted on published historical rock inscriptions of the region. At the end, three annexures namely the copies of Gemur Documents, Gemur Gonpa Chham-yig (Chham Dance Book) and Rock inscriptions have been incorporated.

It is hoped that this will serve as a guide for serious scholars and researchers in carrying out detailed research in the respective field and would be found useful to the lay visitors particularly the tourists during their visit to the valley. At the same time, it may also kindle the desire in the inhabitants of this valley to know more about their heritage and to put in their efforts in preserving it.

Last but not the least, the authors are grateful to Lama Chhering Angial of Sarang who is very kind in sparing a copy of the Chham-yig of the Gemur gonpa for inclusion in this monograph and also verifying the identity of some of the images of the gonpa; Gelong Phunchog of Gemur Phyima for making available of the historical documents and other art objects belonging to Lama Tanzin Paldan; and Shri Tsewang Samphel also of Gemur Phyima for lending copies of the photographs of the images of Tanzin Paldan and other image and Mani-lakhor. The authors are grateful to Shri Thinley Shashni of Tinno Gompapa for translation and typing of the Historical Documents pertaining to Lama Tanzin Paldan which have been returned from Gelong Phunchog of Gemur Phyima. We record sincere appreciation to our families for helping of and on while compiling the materials. We are also thankful to Shri Rakesh Goel of M/S Kaveri Books, New Delhi for taking up of publication of this monograph.

Chhering Dorje
Kullu

Tobdan
Kullu

Contents

1 Introduction

Lahul, as known by various names such as Garza, Garja, Garsha, Karja, Swangla, etc. by its local inhabitants, and Lahul by the outsiders is located on the northern region of Indian Himalaya. It has three valleys, viz. Chandra, Bhaga and Chandra-Bhaga. Chandra Valley is locally known as Rangloi and Gundhla. Khoksar is the first village of the valley from the side of Rohtang. Most of the settlements are located on the right bank and go up to its junction with Bhaga at Tandi. The Bhaga valley starts from the south-western foot of the Baralacha pass and the valley becomes wider from Darcha and up to its junction with Chandra at Tandi. It is divided into two parts. The upper portion of Bhaga valley from the village Darcha to Karing is locally known as Stod and beyond that Gaar. The inhabitants of sTod know it as Punan. The combined rivers of Chandra and Bhaga i.e., Chandra-Bhaga is popularly known as Pattan.

So far as advent of Buddhism in Lahul is concerned, the available evidences reveal that the Indian Buddhism arrived in Lahul quite early and it has left a number of evidences. Gandhala or Gandhola, Ghanḍhāḥr and Guru Ghantal is one of the most ancient Buddhist shrine in Lahul. The scholars in the field trace its origin from the Sanskrit word Gandhalaya from Bodhgaya. The second such standing monument is the temple of Triloknath. There are several other evidences testifying the fact. The area above the site of Gandhala monastery is named as Drilbu Ri (*dril-bu ri*), Bell Mountain and is one of the well-known pilgrimage site and is highly revered by the local populace, meditators and pilgrims and is worshipped as the natural form of Chakrasamvara and Vajravarahi in union. The spiritual power of Lahul, known as Garsha Khandroling, lies in its sacred trinity of Drilbu Ri 'Bell Mountain', Phakpa and Markul Devi. These sites form the Three *Vajra*s of right body, speech and mind. Drilbu Ri Mountain is associated with Chakrasamvara, the enlightened body of Buddha. The other sites of the trinity are Phakpa Temple in Triloknath, associated with Avalokitesvara, the enlightened speech, and Markul Devi Temple in Udaipur, associated with Vajravarahi, the enlightened mind. There is also reference to the site in the documents of the times of the Kullu king Pratap Singh (1539-84) and Prabat Singh (1584-1618). A long song in the praise of it is found mentioned in the Mahatmya of Gandhola Monastery. Therefore, the Drilbu Ri is regarded as a self-created *mChod rten* and is said to be the seat of *Siddha* Drilbu-pa. After finishing the *kora*, circumambulation, around Drilbu Ri, it seemed natural to visit the other two places, Triloknath and Udaipur, as a continuation of the pilgrimage experience. There also exists an ancient carving of a female deity on a boulder near the site of the monastery, belonging to the period of Indian Buddhism, which in the tradition here is named as Dolma Chhudong, image of 'Tara, below which is supposed flowing a stream of water'. Drilbu Ri was a major Tantric site and located on a pilgrimage route, many *Siddhas* including the great Indian master Mahasiddha Ghanta-pa (Drillbu-pa) meditated here.

The discovery of copper vase or *lota* from the site retrieved in 1857 by Major Hay, a British Political agent, is considered to be evidence of Buddhist monks' cells being located in a cave monastery at that time. The frieze on the vase denotes a chariot procession and is considered to be one of the oldest examples of metalwork. It is now kept in the British Museum, London. This *lota* was dated originally to the second-third century CE but now after thorough research in the field, the date has been revised to 1st century BCE. Thus it clearly shows that Buddhism was prevalent in this area. It is also said that the damaged marble head of Avalokitesvara was also found from the site just near the junction of the rivers Chandra and Bhaga. This figure is by far the finest of all the stray Gupta sculptures of the seventh-eighth centuries traced in Himachal Pradesh. However the experts in the field assigned it to eighth century CE. This image is now lost to big thieves and a crude imitation has been kept in guard in the new Thubcholing Gompa. There is also a black stone image of the goddess Vajreśvarī (*rdo rje lha mo*), and a wooden statue of the Buddha. Ghandhala was highly revered as a meditation center as well as a pilgrimage site by the *Siddhas* who practiced Vajrayana. The sacredness of this place is highly praised by Gyalwa rGod tshangpa (1189-1258 CE).

In Lahul the existing Buddhist establishments got strengthened and slowly adapted to Tibetan Buddhism and they escaped from extinction. Evidence of existence of Tibetan Buddhism in Lahul becomes available from the time of Rinchen Zangpo, eleventh century. Two monasteries of Gumrang and Zholing in Lahul are attributed to Rinchen Zangpo. The successive new sects spread to Lahul as and when they appeared. During the medieval period the masters of the Doctrine from the neighboring areas of Ladak and Zanskhar helped in founding monasteries in Lahul. The Brugpa lineage continued to flourish here, with Gandhala as the central monastery in Lahaul. In the latter half of the nineteenth century, Brugpa spiritual leaders of Bhutan sent Lama Tashi Tenphel to Gandhala to guide and teach Lahulis. This brought about a revitalization, because at his leadership, monasteries were restored, rituals improved, and gompas beautified with paintings. He himself did or trained others to do. It is said that all the sacred deities, *mandalas*, and Brugpa lineage holders at Gandhala were painted by Lama Tashi Tenphel in 1870 CE. In 1949, Tagna Rinpoche, Ngawang Dorje (1920-2010), undertook pilgrimage to Garzha as well as to see Brugpa Gonpas. He found that the gonpa founded by his predecessors had become dilapidated and take up renovation of the same which took him two years. Apart from the above, the well-known Brugpa Monasteries in Lahul are: Kardang, Shashur, Tayul and Gemur.

In the present work, an attempt has been made to highlights the Buddhist archaeological remains in the form of monasteries, rock-engraved sculptures, *mani*-walls, *mchod rtens*, inscriptions engraved on rocks, etc. located in sTod, the upper portion of Bhaga valley. The pre-Buddhist religious practices and traditions of worshipping the local deities known as *Lha* have not been included in the present study. The present field work of the area by the authors will help as guide to the future serious researchers in the field.

2 Gemur Monastery and its Subsidiary Shrines

1. Gemur Monastery, Gemur

Gemur Gonpa — Monastery of Gemur — as is popularly known Gemur Monastery, or the monastery of village Gemur, is situated at midway between Karing and Jispa in the upper Bhaga valley, towards Darcha, the last village of Lahul, at a distance of about 20 km from Kyelang, the headquarters of the District Lahul & Spiti. Locally it is famous as Gemur Gonpa and in literature it is written as dGe-sMon gSam-bstan Chos-gling. The monastery can be reached from two ways. For those coming from the side of Kyelang, one has to take the branch road at the ridge after crossing Shiti Lumpa or Nallah before reaching Kolong village. The route passes through the villages of Kolong, Khangsar and Meh. The other route to the site is from the National Highway after crossing the bridge over Chatsi Dokpo at Gemur and walking up for about 20 minutes.

The present monastery is located at a solitary place on a slope at a site called Chhag-tsal-gang just above the village Gemur. This monastery is one of the most easily accessible and is one of the richest monasteries in the entire Lahul valley. This monastic complex comprises of imposing building structure, out-houses for lamas, a separate community kitchen, a large courtyard (*Chham-ra*) for playing the *Chham* dance with a high flat staff called *dar-chha* in the center, public conveyance, huge *mchod-rten* and an inscribed *Mane*-wall, etc.

Nomenclature and the place of founding: The gonpa has no *chhags-rabs* or a written record about its foundation. The existing literary name of the gonpa is 'Gemon Samtan Chos-ling' (*dge-smon bsam-gtan chos gling* = Happy Meditation Land of the Doctrine). It is known that earlier the monastery was known as sMes-kyi-dgon-pa and was situated at a higher place in Meh village. Reference to this monastery is found mention in a votive document of the time of

Parbat Singh (1584-1608 CE), as recorded by A.H. Francke from a *chaitya*, a commemorative of death of a Jo, chief of Hayar household of the village Karing in sTod, from where a nun belonging to the sMes gonpa joined in the funeral ceremony.

The Faith supported: Then a new monastery, named as Samtan Chos-ling was built on a more spacious place on the other side of the seasonal rivulet locally known by the name Gonpa-*lumpa* or *nallah*. The monastery was a fine model of a representative, brief and clean establishment dedicated to the Brug-pa bKa'brgyud-pa sect and it belonged to the *gzhung-'brug* (Middle *'brug*) branch of the *Brug-pa* sub-sect, also known as Brug-pa bKa'brgyud, of the greater school of *Kar'gyud* which was founded by 'Gro-mgon gTsangpa rgya-ras (1161-1211 CE) who is considered to be a *sprul-pa*, a manifestation of Naropa (956-1040 CE), an Indian saint. He is believed to have visited and lived in Zanskar and Ladakh. Gyalwa rGod-tshang-pa (1189-1258), a great scholar, belonged to this lineage, visited Jalandhara i.e. Kangra. He also stayed here in Lahul for quite some time. His lineage is of the same line as Brug-pa Kargyud but he founded a branch out of it of his own named as *sTod 'brug*, the Upper *Drug*. His pupil, Urgyanpa Dharma-seng-ge rNamgyal (1223-1303 CE) far exceeded his fame. He went on pilgrimage through Lahul crossing Jalandhara and visited Urgyan i.e. Uddiyana (Swat valley in Pakistan), the birthplace of Guru Padmasambhava, and came to be designated as the first Urgyanpa.

History of Its Foundation: It is commonly told in the area that Gemur monastery was built by a local lama Tanzin Paldan (bsTan-'dsin dPal-ldan) of the household, 'Gemur Phyima' of the village 'Gemur. He went to Tibet and came back as a scholar of *"hBrug-pa bkargyud"*. The period of his life is not known but there are some estimates about it. Dr. Tashi Paljor, a scholar of the area belonging to the village of 'Bog, places him at about 300 years ago. Late Shri Tanzin Chhakdor, another scholar from the area, considered his time prior to that of Tag-tshang Raspa. Sonam Angdui, a leading lama of the gonpa, tells that Lama Tanzin Paldan was inspired by sTag-tshang Raspa and he selected the site by the manner of mystical casts and founded the monastery. sTag-tshang Raspa (1574-1651CE) stayed in Lahul for about a complete year. In sTod he stayed at Khangsar and Darcha before his departure to Uddiyana in 1615 CE. But there is no reference about his visit to this monastery. However all the successive sTag-tshang Raspa visited from time to time across the centuries, spending weeks or months. They gave teachings and blessings in the three valleys of Lahul. Their holy presence is fervently worshipped in several gonpas and this monastery is especially related to him. It is also told that the *Chham* dance in this gonpa was introduced at the time of sTag-tshang Raspa and the masks and the dress of *chham* were provided by him.

Tanzin Paldan perhaps shifted the site of the monastery to a virgin, open and much spacious place. This is the same place from where the present monastery was established. The place was given the holy name as Samtan Chos-ling and the same name was assigned to the monastery also. Before shifting the monastery to the present site which serves the whole region of sTod, the religious services on the death of a person, etc. was obtained from Chukutsi Gonpa of Khangsar. There is the metal *mandala* of *Mi-'khrugs-pa*, Akshobhya, which is carried along the funeral processions. It is said that it was taken from this monastery. As regards the period of Tanzin Paldan we have another more factual source which enables us to approach the actual time much closer. Lama Rigzin Karayogma, a senior Lama, who also visited Tibet for his higher studies, tells that Tanzin Paldan was disciple of Thinley Shingta, the 7th Drugchen (1718-1766 CE), a great scholar with several religious books in his credit and was instrumental in establishing several monasteries. He was protector of both Nyingma and Kargyud followings. Hence the period of Tanzin Paldan can be placed approximately between 1730-1790 CE and the construction of the Gemur Monastery taken place sometimes around 1770s. In the year 1870, the 2nd Jamgon Trulku Tashi Tenphel of Ladakh (1820-1890 CE) visited this area and as well as the monastery and initiated the overhauling and renovating the building.

Historical Documents and other antiquarian remains of Tanzin Paldan: Lama Tanzin Paldan, belonging to the family of Gemur Phyma, had got built the Gemur monastery. However, there is no other source giving any information about him and his life. The clay image of this great Teacher is enshrined in the row along with other images in the Du khang of the monastery. On its pedestal, there is an inscription in golden letters which reads as *'mkhas grub bstan-'dsin dpal ldan la namo'*, 'reverence to the scholar and *siddha* Tanzin Paldan'. The inscription indicates that he was a scholar who also accomplished the practice of meditation.

Incidentally eighteen old documents along with religious scriptures, three *thangkas* and other religious instruments including small *damru, ghanta* and wooden blocks were retrieved from the house of Tanzin Paldan (*bstan-'dsin dpal ldan*) through Gelong Phunchog, one of his great, great great-grandson. These antiquarian remains or documents are safely kept in a leather covered bamboo box along with the historical documents found in two finely finished leather purses (Pls.1-3).

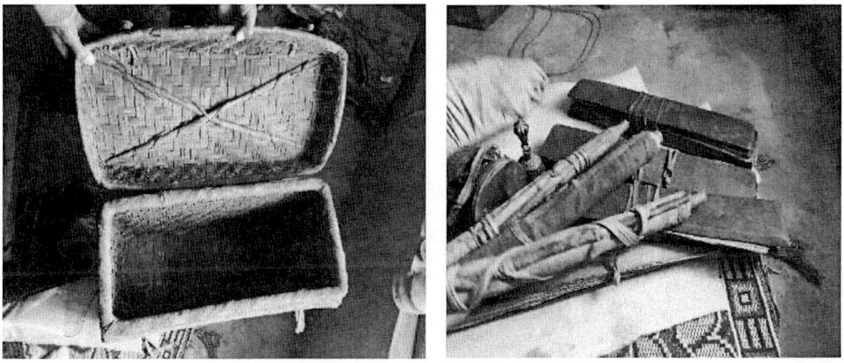

Pl. 1 : Leather covered bamboo box containing antiquarian remains of Lama Tanzin Paldan

Pl. 2 : Leather purse where documents were kept, wooden blocks, damru and ghanta

Pl. 3 : Thang-ka depicting Sadaksari Lokesvara; Vajradhara; twelve-armed Akshobhyavajra

His another clay image and also that of Chakrasamvara and *mani-lagkhor* is at present under active worship in the house of late Kalzang Jorge through Tsewang Samphel, one of the great,great, great-grand-son of Tanzin Paldan (Pl. 4). It is said that these images were shifted from his meditation chamber in the vicinity of the gonpa immediately after the avalanche in 1979.

Pl. 3 : Clay image of Lama Tanzin Paldan and Chakrasamvara; Mani-Lagkhor

The documents referred above are written in *phra-yig,* cursive writing, by different authors. Some of them are duly stamped at the close of the matter, perhaps authenticating the document. Some of these are run to a full page and some have only two lines. A few of them are dated but they give only date and month. Name of Tanzin Paldan is found written in four documents but it gives no clue for his identification or period or any kind of notable activity. There are references to some other Teachers like Rinpoche but they give no further information. In general the documents record the receipt of money, books, performance of worship rites, going to Tibet, etc. and nothing substantial can be found. Among them one document is written by Tashi Tanphel (1811-1875), the 2nd Jamgon Trulku of Tagna Monastery of Ladakh about Gemur gonpa and it is fully dated equivalent to 1887 (Pl. 5). Tashi Tanphel was a great learned Teacher from Ladakh and worked in the monasteries in Lahul for several years. The Original Text Document is reproduced here.

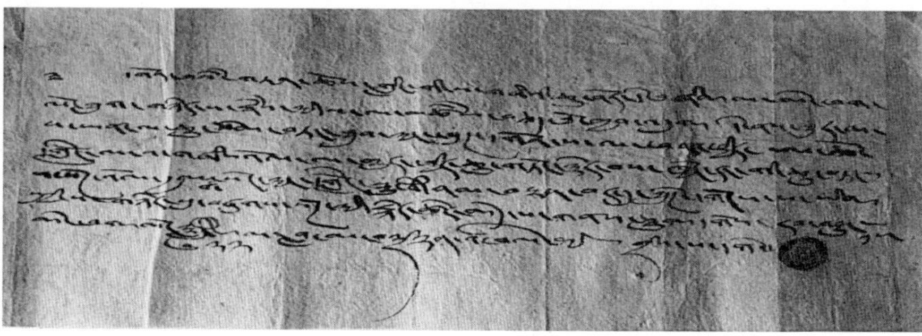

Pl. 5 : Historical documents

Transliteration

༈དགོན་བསམ་གཏན་ཆོས་གླིང་གི་ས་གཞིའི་ཆུ་ནོར་དེ་བཞིན་ལ་མོ་ཁག་ལོ་ཐུག་གཉེར་པ་རྣམས་ཀྱི་ས་ལ་མཚམས་ བཅད་ཐོ་རྒྱབ་འདུག། དེ་ནས་ཐུར་མ་ས་ཡན་ལ་ཆུ་ཙམ་བཏང་ཐུབ་ཀྱང་། ཐུགས་དགོན་པ་ལ་ཕན་ ཕྱིར། ཨ་ཅོ་དགེ་སློང་ལ་ ས་གཞི་དགོན་ལ་སྒྱུར་ཕྱིར་ཆུ་གཏོང་ཟེར་བས་ཁོང་(ཁྱོད་)རང་གི་ཆུ་བཏངས་ས་སོགས་འོལ་རྒྱལ་བ་སོང་ཀྱང་དགེ་སློང་སྨ་ ཚེ་ནམ་བརྟན་བར་དུ་ཐུགས་རྗེ་དགོངས་པ་ཡིན། སྤྱི་ས་གཉེར་སུ་བཞུགས་སོགས་ཀྱི་སྐོར་ཆེར་(ཆོར་)མེད་པ་གནས་ཙུག་ (བཅུག་)དགོས། རབ་འབྱུང་༡༥(མེ་ཕག་ལོ་ཟླ་༤ཚེས་༢༢ལ་བླ་མ་བཀྲིས་བརྟན་འཕེལ་གྱིས་བྲིས་པ་དགེ།།(༡༢)

Translation

The source of the water (water asset) of the site for (construction of) the monastery of bSam-gtan Chos-gling [and the site] has been demarcated and the boundary pillars have been raised by the important, annual, regular caretakers. The land from this place, the point of source of the water, down up to the original land, the land which is being cultivated, should be irrigated extensively. As much as water is given here, it will be beneficial in the long run for the [building of] monastery. Brother Gelong, the monk, has been advised to irrigate in order to convert the land making capable of constructing the monastery over it. As he will irrigate the land, it will get changed with good growth of grass. He will keep on doing so till he remains healthy and fit, till he becomes too old. Anybody may remain caretaker of this common crop of grass, it should be left as it is. No turn of the villagers should be fixed for looking after and regular irrigation of the grassland. This document was written on the 22nd day of the 6th month of the fire-hog year of the 15th cycle, accordingly C.E. 1887.

These original text documents in *phra-yig* have been transliterated in to *dbu-bchan* characters and also typed by Thinley Shashni.The copies of the remaining original documents with their transliterations are annexed (**Annexure I**).

The present premises of the Monastery: In the year 1979, this monastery was again washed away in the avalanche and a nun, popularly known as Abey Palzey from Jispa Melagpa, also lost her life. Efforts had been made to retieve all the valuables and antiquarian remains from the site.Then it was decided to shift to a new site. Accordingly the site, locally known as Chhag-tsal-gang was selected for construction of a new building of the monastery. The remains of ruins of the structures of the monastery can still be seen at the old site and the surrounding agricultural land of the monastery is left unused.

The present monastery is located on a slope surrounded by a large vacant land of its own (Pl. 6). Those coming up from the main road one first meets its m*Chod rten* and a *Mane*-wall, a block of stones over which are kept the inscribed stones, mostly with the sacred formula *'om mani padme hum'*, (= Om, jewel on the Lotus). Then one enters the premises of the gonpa.

Pl. 6 : View of the Monastery from south-east and from top

The construction of the new building of the monastery was started on a new safe site under the overall supervision and guidance of Late Venerable Lama Ngawang Thinley (Ngag-dbang prin-les) of Rangrik, the then head of the monastery. He was instrumental in designing the architecture as well as supervising the construction project of the new Monastic building from foundation till completion (Pl. 7).

Pl. 7 : Ven. Lama Ngag-dbang Thinley, the founder of the present monastery

The present monastery is a three storeyed structure on a high raised platform and facing east. The surviving valuables and images were shifted to the present newly built building. The existing literary name of the Gonpa is 'Gemon Sam-tan Chos-glin' (*dGe-sMon gSam-bstan Chos-gling*). On the lowest story are the sacred establishments of the monastery and the middle story is used for the informal gatherings and sitting of the lamas and guests. On the third, the uppermost floor, one part is maintained as a set for the stay of visiting lama guests, called Zim-chung (*gzim-chung*), small sleeping room. The remaining part is the Kangyur Lha Khang. The core of the lower story is divided into two parts: Du-khang (*'du-khang*) and inner Lha-khang. In the Du-khang, there are placed statues of the class of the superior mortal beings, the high ranking historical personages belonging to the sect. In the Lha-khang, it enshrines two large statues of Vajradhara and Vajra-varahi, the benevolent divine beings, the chief god and goddess of the sect.

Thematically the establishment comprises six sections viz., *Chham-ra,* dancing Hall, attached to the main building; *sGo-khang,* antechamber, the entrance; *Du-khang* or *Du-khang chhed-mo,* the assembly hall; *Lha-khang*, the sanctum; *Kangyur Lha-khang*; and *mGon-khang*, the chamber of the guardian deities.

A. Chham-ra: Crossing the gate one enters the open and uncovered courtyard surrounded on three sides by the covered verandah and on one side of which on the left is situated the gonpa. The courtyard, which is used as such during the normal days is designed especially for playing the *Chham* dance during the festival or T*sheshu* (held in around middle of July every year) and is named as *Chham-ra,* courtyard for playing *chham.* In the centre of the *Chhamra* is placed two flag-poles with prayer flags, *Darchen* (*dar-chhen,* big flag) on a raised square platform. On its top is mounted the *khatam-kha* (Pl. 8).

On the south east side is the *mchhod-khang*, the room for offering prayer lamps. During the *Chham* the lamas reciting the books sit at one corner on the east wall on a raised platform. Fine stone carved slabs depicting figures of Buddhas in low relief and inscriptions in Bhoti characters are fixed on this east wall. These are prayers from the book *ltung-gshags,* confession of sin and thirty five deities who are worshipped in the book are also engraved on stone and laid on the wall at the same place. Names of the deities are in Bhoti script. Some of the sketches have become obliterated.

Pl. 8 : Chhamra or the courtyard and sitting arrangement for lamas in front of east wall facing the main entrance

The viewers of Tsheshu festival sit in the vacant places along the covered verandah and the flat top roof rest on beam and rafters supported by wooden circular columns placed at equal distance. *Tshechu* is an important event in the annual calendar of the monastery and it is called Tshe-bdag *Tshe-bchu* or *tshe-shu* of Tshe-bdag introduced by sTag-tshang Raspa. It is celebrated on the nineteenth day of the fifth month of Tibetan calendar year. The main purpose of this sacred performance of *chham* dance is to bestow good health, subjugate disease and conquer evil spirits. The festivities start four or five days earlier and rituals are performed on a daily basis in the monastery. Lamas also practices *chham* dance with the *chhamspon* to oversee the various logistical and ecclesiastical needs. This event is an attraction for the locals as well as the tourists who gather for the festivals.

B. sGo-khang: Access to the entrance porch, sGo-khang, is through a flight of about a dozen masonry stairs from the front courtyard. The small porch rests on a decorated beam of the ceiling supported by two wooden columns with decorated capitals. On the right side of it there is the *Mane-Dung-gyur*, the revolving prayer wheel (Pl. 9).

Pl. 9 : View of Go-khang from Chhamra; wheel of life; Mane-Dung-gyur

The paintings on the entrance wall depict the figures of gods of directions, two figures on either side of the entrance of the Du-khang (Pls.10-11). Dhritarastra serves as the guardian in the East and he protects the land and living beings and he wears various kinds of celestial robes. He is shown holding a *vina* with both his hands. He is depicted as white. Virudhaka is the great king of the south and resides in the middle of Sumeru Mountain. He is red in colour and holding a sword in his right hand while his left hand rests on his knee. Virupaksha is the great king of the west. He is the lord of Nagas and is shown in red colour holding a spear of three points, his left fist rests on his knee. His symbol is a mchod rten in his left hand. Vaisravana is the great king of the north. He is the lord of *yaksas* and the lord of wealth and adorned with precious jewels, besides the paintings of *srid-pa'i khorlo*, the wheel of existence. These paintings were done in recent years by Angchug, Pon from Sarang village.

Pl. 10 : Dhritarastra &Vaisravana; Dhritarastra

Pl. 11 : Virudhaka and Virupaksha

C. Du-khang: Du-khang or the assembly hall is the main chamber where most of the sculptures, *thangkas*, religious instruments and ceremonial *tormas* and *chhodpas* are properly displayed in wooden shelves (Pls. 12-14). All the monks or lamas used to sit in two rows on either side for recitations from the Holy Scriptures on the occasions of ceremonial performances.. It is rectangular in shape and the ceiling of the roof top rests on four square beams supported by four wooden columns at equidistance and in the center there is an opening for lights etc. Close to the ceiling, a walkway runs all along the top. This is used for hanging *thangkas* and for light from top.

Pl. 12 : Panoramic view of the interior of Du-khang

The wooden columns and capitals are beautifully carved and painted with enamel paints. The flooring is of wooden planks.The entire central or west wall is covered with wooden showcases for accommodating the antiquarian remains of the monastery in the form of clay as well as metal sculptures of the high ranking historical figures belonging to the sect and other day to day ritual artefacts and instruments. The religious scriptures are placed in the bookshelves alphabetically. On the left side facing the west is the seat for high ranking Rinpoche. While in the center is the raised altar for offerings during periodical religious ceremonies. At the head of the rows in the middle is placed a *mChod rten* of a precious metal studded with precious jewels, some of which were stolen some years back.

Pl. 13 : Close view of Du-khang

Pl. 14 : Precious metal mchod-rten; wooden mchod rten; rDo-rje or namchag

The row of statues: The clay image of Buddha is central figure of the *Du-khan* and the other images include Shamnatha identified it with sTagtshang Raspa, Kunkhyen Padma Karpo, Padmasambhava, Zhabdung Ngawang Namgyal, Lama Tashi Tanphel, mKhas grub Tanzin Paldan and sTagtshang Raspa, almost of equal height of about three feet. The figures are detailed below starting from the left side of the viewer (Pls.15-17).

Pl. 15 : Clay images of Shambhunatha; Padma Karpo; Padmasambhava

The image of Shamnatha with a round white hat is typical of the Indian ambivalent *yogis* of the *natha* sect, actually represents sTagtshang Raspa. The image is shown seated on a plain pedestal. His right is in *bhumisaparsamudra* while his left hand is in the lap holding vase. He wears a monk's dress. The same statue is found in Hemis in Ladakh and is known by the same name. In 1973 a very senior Lama of the monastery, Lama Wangchug, who also was Onpo, astrologer, gave its name as Shamunatha and identified it with sTagtshang Raspa. According to the travelogue of sTagtshang Raspa while he was on pilgrimage to Uddiyana he was ordained into *Natha Panth* and he was given the name as Shamnatha.

There is a painting on the wall at Hemis which is named as Shamnatha. There is also a prayer book where the Master is named as Shamnath. It is said that the statues were made by Tashi Tanphel. All the statues cannot be assigned to his workmanship. Shamnatha may belong to an older period sometime after the death of the Master and may be of the same period as is found in Hemis named as Shamunatha.

Kunkhyen Padma Karpo (*kun-mkhyen pad-ma dkar-po*) was the fourth Gyalwang Brug-pa, the head of the Brug-pa lineage (1527—1592 CE). He was the most learned of all the Gyalwang Brug-pas. He authored a number of scholarly works. His two important historical works are *'Brug chhos-byung* and *Lho chhos-byung* (History of Brug-pa and History of Lho Brug). There are about two dozen volumes of the works of this Teacher in the Gonpa library. Here the image is shown wearing the usual monk's dress and hat. His right hand is shown in *bhumisaparsamudra* (touching the earth) while his left hand in the lap holding vase.

The image of Padmasambhava is shown in the middle row which appears to be much older than others. He is shown seated on a high raised decorated lotus pedestal and wearing the usual monk's dress and cap. His right hand is in front of the chest in *budhasramanamudra* holding *vajra* and left hand in the lap holding bowl over which is the vase. *Khatavanga* is shown on the left side. On his left is the image of Lama Tanzin Paldan, the founder of this monastery, Lama Tashi Tamphel and another image of sTag-tshang Raspa. These images are shown wearing the monks dress and the caps.

Tanzin Paldan (*mkhas grub bstan-'dsin dpal ldan*) was from Gemur village and he was a great scholar and *siddha*. This is known from an inscription written in gold on the pedestal of his throne which reads *'mkhas grub bstan-'dsin dpal-ldan la namo'* - obeisance to the scholar and *siddha* Tanzin Paldan. He strengthened the cultural relations with the Hemis monastery and monastic activities of Gemur gonpa are being looked after from time to time by the representatives of that monastery.

Tashi sTanphel (1811-1875 CE) from Ladakh was enrolled as a novice at Hemis Monastery at an early age and was formally enthroned as the incarnation of Trulku Karma Tanzin of sTagna monastery. He belonged to Lho Drug following, slightly different from gZhung-drug. He was instrumental in propagation of Brug-pa tradition in Ladakh, Zanskar and its neighboring regions. On the corner of the southern wall there is a statue of the 4th Jamgon Trulku Ngawang Donyo Dorje, the sTagna Rinpochhe (1922-2010).

The image of sTagtshang Raspa is said to be a later addition and was done in around 1940. If this statement is true, then the statue cannot be said to represent the first teacher of the line but is generic representing the lineage of the Teacher. 1st sTag tshang Raspa was Ngag dbang rgya-mtsho or Shamnatha (1574-1651), the founder of Hemis Gonpa. He was followed by 2nd Tag-tshang Raspa 'mTsho skyes rdor-rje (1655-), 3rd Tagtsang Raspa' bDe-chhen rdo-rje (1730-), 4th Tag-tshang Raspa Aatsarya Tsanchen (1805-), 5th Tag-tshang Raspa Drodul Padma Lingpa (sTag tshang lnga pa 'gro 'dul gling-pa) (1875-1941), and 6th Tag tshang Raspa Ngag-dbang sTanzin Chos kyi nyi-ma (1942-).

Pl. 16 : Lama Tanzin Paldan; Lama Tashi Tamphel; sTag-tshang Rinpoche, all in clay

Zhabdung Ngawang Namgyal (*Zhabs-drung ngag-dbang rnam-rgyal)* (1594-1651CE) was born in Tibet as the son of the Drukpa lineage-holder Mipham Tanpa'i Nyima. On his father's side Ngawang Namgyal descended from the family line of Tsangpa

Pl. 17 : Zhabdung Ngawang Namgyal (?); Tagna Rinpoche; Buddha (?); Avalokitesvara Padmapani

Gyare (1161-1211CE), the founder of the Drukpa Lineage. Ngawang Namgyal was enthroned as the 18th Drukpa and recognized there as the immediate reincarnation of the 4th Drukchen, the "Omniscient" Kunkhyen Padma Karpo. He was the founder of the Lho Drug sub-sect.

All these statues of historical figures are shown seated in meditative postures. They are all almost of equal height of about 0.90m. All the informants agree to relate that these clay statues in the row were set up by Tashi Tanphel whose period of active activities in Lahul is the decade around 1870s. Except the two, Shamnath and Padmasambhava, all other statues wear the same type of red cap which is called *Gom-zha* (*sgom-zhva* = meditation cap). This is found used with the monks of *Drukpa* following. The round big and circular *zhva-nag*, black cap, is worn here during the ceremonial performances by the *Chhampon*, the leader of the *Chham* dance.

In front of these images are seen the statues of four armed Avalokiteshvara and Buddha Sakyamuni in metal (Pl. 18). Both the deities are shown seated in *vajraparyankasana* on lotus pedestals. Front two arms of Avalokitesvara are shown in *namaskaramudra* while in the upper right hand he holds *mala* and in the left a full blown lotus. He wears elaborately decorated crowns on his head. While the right hand of Sakyamuni is shown in *bhumisaparsamudra* and the left hand is on lap holding *patra*. Besides the above, three miniature images are also kept above these images in the wooden alcoves.

Pl. 18 : Metal image of four-armed Lokesvara and Sakyamuni

Thang-ka paintings: Thang-ka painting is one of the great arts and is rich not only in its iconography, religious content and stylistic development, but also in terms of the materials and skills that the painters and their patrons lavished upon it. This monastery has a good collections of *thang-kas* on cloth depicting various deities of Buddhist pantheon of which the only displayed in the walls of Du khang deserve special mention are Mahakala, Jag-pa melen, Jambal Tshe-bdag, Vajrasattva, Amitabha, Padmasambhava, Mahakala, Avalokitesvara, Vajrakilaya with other deities, and *mandalas* of Mahakala and Tshe-bdag, etc. (Pls. 19-21).

Pl. 19 : Thang-kas depicting Vajrasattva; Vajrakilaya. Amitabha and Mahakala with other deities

Pl. 20 : Thang-kas depicting Padmasambhava; Mahakala; Avalokitesvara; and Vajrakilaya with other deities

Pl. 21 : Thang-ka Mandala depicting Gonbo and Tsedak

The Wall Paintings: The entire inner side walls are decorated with recently executed paintings depicting various scenes of the life of Buddhas and other Bodhisattvas. Some paintings of the deities are done on clothes and are pasted on the wall (Pls. 22-23). These paintings contain the depiction of deities, scholars and great lamas of Brug-pa lineage, some of them as they are known in the *mandalas* or groups, such as: *gnas gtan bchu drug, ltung gshags, rgyal chhen bde bzhi, dkargyud gser phreng,* etc.

Pl. 22 : Murals showing Padmasambhva in the centre

On the northern side of the wall, on the right as we enter, in the Du- khang, the paintings were done by a Lama painter from Karsha

Gonpa, Zanskar sometime in between 1980 and 1990. The painting on the southern side is older.

Pl. 23 : Murals on the walls showing deities of Buddhist pantheon

Other paintings in the Du-khang are of the eight forms of Guru Padmasambhva, Akshobhya, Amitayus, Manjusri, Tara, Sitatara, Yellow Tara, Saraha, Hayagriva, Dorrje Leg-pa, Ekajati, Mi-la ras-pa, Buddha, Vaisravana, Khretrapal, Tshering-ma, Mahakala, Vajrakila, Chaturbhuja Aryavalokitesvara, etc. On the left side are the deities of Nyingma-pa, sixteen great *sthavira*, Amitabha, etc.

D. Lha-khang: On the back of the Du-khang is another Lha-khang which is very narrow and rectangular in shape. Access to this Lha Khang is from the left corner of the central wall of the Du khang. In front of the central wall is the altar where enshrined the two clay images, Vajradhara (*rdo-rje phyang*) and Vajrayogini, 'Marichi Vajravarahi' (*rdo-rje phag-mo*) and smaller or miniature images on high raised pedestal in row (Pls.24-25). The former is about one and half storey high and the latter one storey. Vajradhara is shown seated in *vajrasana* on a high raised lotus pedestal. He is in blue colour holding *vajra* in his right hand and bell in the left, both crossed over his chest. He is wearing five pointed decorated crown in hid head.

Pl. 24 : Vajradhara (rDo-rje chhang) and Marichi Vajravarahi (rDo-rje Phag-mo)

Pl. 25 : Sadakasari Lokesvara and metal amulet, Amitayus?, Buddha and namcuwangdan

While the image of Vajrayogini, 'Marichi Vajravarahi' is shown on his left in red colour. She is in standing in dancing posture and has two arms holding in her right *vajra* with raised index finger, and in the left *kapala* and *khatavanga*. She is shown single-face with three eyes and dishevelled hair and stands naked marked with six auspicious symbols in the *pratyalidha* attitude tramples upon the gods Bhairava and Kalaratri. She is shown wearing a garland of human heads. The goddess is a beautiful example of an elegant Kashmiri model in clay, studded with precious stones, gold and silver with its lovely elongated round limbs, shapely breast and elegant and sophisticated posture. On the west of the Vajravarahi there are four wooden *mchod-rtens* in a row on low platform. In front of Vajravarahi there is Sadakasari Lokesvara with six arms in the aspect of *'gro-ba drug 'grol*, Liberator of six kinds of beings, , Amitayus, Buddha, all in clay, metal amulet and *namcuwandan* in stone. These images are attributed to twelfth century CE.

The side walls of this chamber are profusely decorated with paintings depicting various scenes of Buddhist pantheons. On the left side are the deities of Nyingma, sixteen great *sthavira*, Amitabha, etc. It is said that these paintings were done by a Lama painter from Karsha gonpa, Zanskar in between 1980 and 1990 (Pl. 26).

Pl. 26 : Wall painting showing various deities of recent periods

E. Kangyur Lha-khang: In the first floor, the Lha khang is square on plan and it contains Tanjur, Kangyur and other texts are arranged in wooden showcases on the north and west walls besides numerous clay as well as metal images enshrined in the alcoves (Pl. 27). The ceiling of this chamber rests on a single beam supported by two square wooden columns. The wooden capitals are profusely decorated with modern enamel paints. The clay images displayed in this chamber on the north wall include Buddha in *bhumisparsa-mudra*, Padmasambhava, eleven-headed Avalokitesvara (*spyan-ras-gzigs*), Padmasambhava, sGam-po-pa, Marpa (chos-kyi-blo-gros), Mi-la-ras-pa, and various other deities in seated positions, all covered with scarf, cloths (Pl. 28).

Pl. 27 : View of the Kangyur Lha khang

Pl. 28 : Clay images showing Mela repa, Marpa, Gampopa, Padmasambhva, Avalokitesvara, Buddha, etc.displayed in Kangyur Lha Khang

The image of Buddha is displayed on the west wall showcase. All the images are displayed in the wooden frames. There are two sets of Kangyur and one set of Tangyur besides several Sungbum, collected works, 24 volumes of the works of Padma Karpo and other important scriptures.

In the outer corridor. of this floor, there is an ancient prayer-wheel (Mani-Dung-gyur) on a low height platform. The abbot's chamber overlooking the courtyard is located on the right side where high ranking lamas of the monastery who are not directly engaged in the rituals and invited guests, etc. are accommodated during festive occasions.

F. mGon khang —The Chamber of Protective Deities: Access to the Gon-khang at the top floor is through wooden stairs from this corridor on the left side of the first floor. It is rectangular in plan. The roof top is rest on two beams supported by four wooden columns. The ceiling as well as the side walls are devoid of any painting. This chamber is in two parts. The space on the back is kept for the tantric practices and houses the terrifying aspects of images of Paldan

Lhamo, Jampel Tse-bdag and four-armed mGonbo (Mahakala), the main protectors or *srungma* of the monastery (Pls. 29-31). The latter two are displayed in the Tsheshu festival. It is said that these images were accomplished by Lama Tamdin of Tinan and Lama Kunga of Kyelang in the second half of the twentieth century. This shrine is usually kept secret and the religious practices are performed on daily basis only by the Lama in-charge of the monastery. Entry to the inner chamber where these deities are enshrined is completely restricted. The front portion is used during keeping masks, dresses of the *chham* dancers during festive occasions.

Pl. 29 : View of the chamber outside mGon-khang where masks are displayed

Pl. 30 : Paldan Lhamo; Mahakala; and Jampel Tse-bdag

Pl. 31 : Jampel Tse-bdag engraved on stone slab and on thanka displayed during Chham dance

There is a *thanka* of Gonpo in black colour drawn in gold which is said to have been prepared by Lama Yontan of village Sumnam in Pattan. On the back of the monastery on the hill side, there is a stone slab depicting a ferocious looking figure of the *srungma,* Jampel Tse-bdag engraved in low relief and is under active worship. He is shown wearing an armour and rides on a horse. The image is worshipped by one of the monk on regular basis till the end of the annual *tseshu* fair. The same figure was depicted on a large *thangka* made of silk by stitching small pieces of silk cloth which was stolen from the monastery sometimes in the year 1960's along with other valuable articles, but efforts have not been made to trace the original as well as other valuables. In its place a new *thanka* of the same figure dedicated to Tse-bdag was prepared by lama painter from Karsha Monastery, Zanskar in around 1977 and is unfurled on the wall overlooking the courtyard on this festive occasion. The present *thangka* about a storey high and the sacred masks of the *chham* dance are also kept in this chamber. However the side chambers on this floor are being used for the purpose of residence or living rooms, stores, etc.

Shing-par-Wood blocks: The monastery has a rich collection of wooden blocks which include 30 blocks relating to *mandala,* 30 of the worship of Paldan Lhamo, 150 of Bardo thodol, 50 of Leu dunma, and some others. It is said that some of the important wooden blocks have been shifted to Ladak.

Tshe-shu (*tshe-bshu*) Chham festival: The ceremony of *Chham* is held three times in the year, although *Tsheshu* is the biggest. One is held in the summer well known as Gemur *Tsheshu.* The second is held in the winter during the time of *Kang-gsol*. The third is also held as *Zhva nag*. The *Tsheshu* festival is held here every year on the nineteenth day of the fifth month of Tibetan calendar year. It is an important festival held annually at the gonpa. It is called *Tse-bdag Tshe-bchu, tshe-shu* of *Tshe-bdag,* a wrathful aspect of Manjusri, the Buddha of wisdom which is said to have been introduced by sTag-tshang Raspa. It is said that he also provided the masks and dress of the dance. The monks assemble about three or four days earlier and are performed based on Gonpa's *Tshe-bdag chham-yig* (**AnnexureII**). *Chham* dance takes place in the open courtyard (*Chhamra*) facing the main entrance. The ceremonial items such as bowls full of water, uncooked rice and butter and incense sticks are placed on the platform in the center of the courtyard. Sitting arrangement for the group of lamas is made on a small space in front of the east wall facing the main entrance of the monastery. A sacrificial offering, a human figure made of dough and is kept on the triangular container over the ground in front of the central platform.

The *chham* dance starts with the solemn entry of the monastic orchestra with clashing cymbals, beating drum and blowing of long trumpets, followed by *Chhams-pon*, the Black Hat dancer holding *rDo-rje* or *vajra* on his right hand and *dril-bu* or *ghanta* on his left hand. He wears a round big and circular *zhva-nag*, black cap during the ceremonial performances. He is the leader of the *chham* dancer and also directs the play and dances around the central pole with slow and solemn movements of legs and hands to the special music of drum, cymbals and wind-trumpets (Pl. 32).

Pl. 32 : Sethang ceremony with the arrival of Chhampon

After turning for a while clockwise around the courtyard, the Black Hat dancer steps upon the square carpet spread out in front of the sacrificial offering, a human figure made of dough. He blesses and dedicates the offerings and then stabs the effigy thrice by means of a miniature weapon. Then again takes a round dancing. This whole section is repeated eight times. Then appears four dancers called *mgo-ma bzhi* in four different colours, wearing wrathful masks with a third eye on their foreheads and their mouths are open with a protruding tongue curled upwards (Pl. 33). The white one is holding *parsu* in his right hand while the yellow coloured one holds rope-like objects in his both hands. The red coloured dancer is holding a chain like object in his right hand while the green coloured holds *ghanta* in his right hand. They dance around the courtyard with quick short steps, while the Black Hat dancer turns round the courtyard with slower and more solemn movements. The four dancers adjust their steps with the Black Hat dancer and then approach the triangular container to stab the dough effigy one by one.

Pl. 33 : Four masked dancer in different colours

Afterwards two *Kha'u* players, *khwata* and *dugpa,* in red and dark green colours and holding flags in blue and red colours in their right hands, enter in the scene and the whole action is repeated (Pl. 34).

Pl. 34. Kha'u players, khwata-dugpa dnacers

Thereafter comes the *sde-brgyad*. This is the principal *chham (gzhung-chham)*. They all dance together and then go in. The eight masked and richly dressed dancers representing a class of gods appear in the scene. The costumes of these dancers are made of applique works and the striking face of a fierce god on their aprons. Each of these eight dancers too turn by turn stab the effigy (Pls. 35-36).

Pl. 35 : Eight dancers (sde-brgyed)

Pl. 36 : Combined group of fifteen dancers

The next *chham* dancers appear on the scene are two *Shva-ba* or deer masked dancers, *pho* and *mo,* male and female in white and yellow colours holding swords in their right hands while the left are shown empty (Pls. 36-37).

Pl. 36 : Entry of two deer masked dancers, Shva Pho and Mo

They dance and go in. Then the *Chham-pon* kneels down on the square carpet and cuts the effigy into pieces and the pieces are thrown in four different directions representing the killing of the enemy of Buddhism and purification of the human soul from the three evils, ignorance, jealousy and hatred. The play ends with a quick dance of victory, after which the dancers retreat in the monastery.

Pl. 37 : Group of twelve chham dancers

Finally, Hwashang, the smiling Buddha, a teacher with his assistant and four *hatukas*, his disciples appear in the scene showing the old method of teaching in schools (Pls. 38-39). This is called *rGya-gi tem-drel*, ceremonial closure with the Chinese performance. It is told that they lived in Tibet for seven generations.

Pl. 38 : Entry of Hwashang-the smiling Buddha with his Hatuka dancers

Pl. 39 : Hatuka dance

In the late evening, *Zor (gtorma) chham* is held outside the monastery by the Black Hat dancers where *torma* (sacrificial effigy made of dough) representing the evil powers destroyed by the head of the Black Hat dancers is burnt.

The Chham dance was seen by PH.Pott in 1952 and some of his photographs illustrating the intricate movements of *chham-yig*, held in the earlier gonpa are now published by Nebesky-Wojkowitz in his book titled *Tibetan Religious Dance*, Mount, The Hague, 1976: 120, plates III & IV (Pl. 43). The some of the published photographs are reproduced here (Pl. 40).

Pl. 40 : Photos of Chham dance in 1952

The next day, on 20th, a *chhoga*, the worship of *tsheshu* is held. This is the dance of Tshe-bdag, Yamantaka symbolizing the victory of the good over the bad and annihilation of the evil spirits.

The Monastic Organization: The ecclesiastic class here is a compact organized community and there is a long range of hierarchical positions occupied by the members. Each of the next stages is considered as higher than the former and each post is held for three years. If at some positions the occupant is more deserving or may be some other reason, he is requested to continue for another term. The initial positions are more laborious. The first entrants in the organization are called *btsun-chung,* junior monks. The pupils have to learn reading and writing privately by adopting a teacher for themselves. There is no formal arrangement for learning and training of the monks. The engagements of the lamas include ceremonies performed at the monastery on various dates of the year; the appointed or selected monks to perform the religious performances at subsidiary shrines and also to serve the people of the area; conduct many religious performances in the villages and at the villagers' houses, etc.

This monastery functions as the main religious establishment and controls subsidiary smaller Gonpas viz., Dartse, Chhukutsi, dZong gonpa, Chos-Khang of Khangsar-Khar and Photang in Jispa. The various other positions assigned to the monks in the monastery are that they function as musicians of which there are two positions; ***Dung-pa,*** one who plays on ***dung,*** the large trumpet and ***rgya-ling-pa,*** one who plays on a smaller trumpet during all the ceremonies. ***mChhod-dpon*** is responsible for preparation of a large number of sacrificial offerings in the form of *gtor-ma, mchhod-pa* and *tshhogs* of *tsampa,* flour of barley or some other. They have to be prepared during the various religious services. ***dKongnyer*** of Gemur gonpa is assigned the duty according to his seniority. His task is cleaning the worship room, to light the prayer lamps, offering water in the metal bowls and emptying them in the evening. He keeps the keys of the gonpa and to show the monastery to the visitors. Maintenance of all the articles such as the statues, articles, etc. is part of his function. ***gZhung gnyer*** is performed by four lamas to look after the works of arrangement of tea, meal, etc. for the lamas and the *Yon-bdag-mo,* landladies, during other performances in the monastery and during the festival of *Tsheshu.* ***rTsis-gnyer*** is assigned to two lamas to keep the account of income and expenditure including the expenditures incurred during ceremonies and to keep record of the property of the monastery and are also responsible for the maintenance and development of the gonpa. ***dBu chhung*** functions with ***dbu-mdsad*** and plays cymbals during ritual functions and to give recitations of the scriptures according to the set rhythm, etc. After three years ***dbu-chhung*** occupies the position of ***dbu-mdsad***. ***dbu-mdsad*** is an important office. He is the second lama after the head lama of the monastery. His attendance is compulsory in the ceremonies at the gonpa and Khar and at the villagers. His function is to play the cymbals and lead the recitation of the scriptures in the ceremonies. Others follow him. Earlier the most able lama was posted in this office. After three years in the event of non-availability of a suitable person his position is continued. He has to function as the Head Lama in the absence of the head lama. **Dartse Lama** is deputed seniority wise on rotation at the monastery at Dartse for three years. ***rDo-rje sLob-dpon*** is the highest rank. He sits at the head of all the lama in the ceremonies. He plays the bell and the *damru*. On the occasion of a death in the villages he has to perform the act of ***pho-ba spar-che*** and the lamas from the Gemur gonpa have to perform the rites. It takes about 39 years of career for a lama in the area. Some of the lamas due to their knowledge and efficiency may be requested to continue the post for another term. The lama who has completed the circle of various positions of the monastery is called *bla-zur*, Lama on the edge.

Dus bzang or holy ceremonies at the Gonpa: The important holy day celebrations performed in this gonpa include *bla-ma mchhod-pa* on 22nd of 3rd month of Tibetan Calendar, and worship of *Dorje-bdag* and *zhabs-brtan* of sTag tshang Raspa; *Tshe-dkyil* on 15th and *mandala* on 16th of 4th month; *chhos-bzhang* on 8th day of 5th month; and *Dampa rigs rgya* on 9th and 10th of 5th month and also prayer is held for sTag tshang Raspa. *lha sde brgyad* or *kalachakra* is worshipped on 22nd of 7th. It is a *Chhoga Dgu-btor on* 7th of 9th month, on 8th *zhung chhog* or *gonpo chhoga* is held and on 9th *Chhoga*. This *torma* is called *dgu-gtor*. Gonbo, Mahakala, *zor chham* is held in which all the lamas come out in black hats which may be of any number, but usually around ten. *dampa rigs brgya, gZhi-khro* in 10 th month. *si(rtsis)-rug rgyab-che*, annual accounting, is done in the 11th month, etc. till the end of the year.

Service Area: The monastery is supported by the residents of the whole of the region of sTod which covers the area from Karing to Darcha in the upper Bhaga valley. The lamas of the monastery provide the necessary religious services of every kind to the people of the area. Lamas are sent from here to the gonpas of Dartse, Chhukutsi, Zong gonpa, Khangsar khar and Photang in Jispa on rotations. The lama sent to Dartse is designated as *Dartse Lama* and others as *Kongnyer*. Except the *Kongnyer* to Photang who is sent for one year, all others are sent for three years.

Yul-phe dus-bzang, the holy days at the villagers: The religious ceremonies performed in the villages and at the houses of the villagers are: *gzhi-khro* or *yul-gzhi khro* or *grong-pa'i zhi-khro*, the ceremony held at the various houses; *sku-rim, skang-gsol, g-yang-khug*, and *Lha-bsang* at the houses of all; *sa-bdag gdon-grol;* worship of *sing-ge-sgra* and Varuna; *mandala-zhima*, in which *Jetsun Dolma* is worshipped; *tshog-le, spyod-tshog; chho-ga* of *'Od-pag-med; gzhi-khro, zhong chhog* on the occasion of a death; *tshe-grub; dkon-mchhog gchig dus; chhi-med rgyan drug; tshe-shu* about the Guru; *Nya-ne nyung-ne; chhos rog-che*, reciting from books like *mdo-dbang; brgyad-stong-pa*, etc. and sometimes the larger books like *Kangyur*.

rGyan-drug mChhog-gnyis (Six Ornaments and two Supreme Ones): There are teachers known as six ornaments and two jewels of the world. The foremost ornaments are Nagarjuna, Aryadeva, Asanga, Vasubandhu, Dignaga and Dharmakirti. The two jewels are Gunaprabha and Sakyaprabha.

dKar-brgyud gser 'phreng (the Golden Rosary of Kargyud, the eminent Teachers of Kargyud Sect): The direct master-disciple transmission of the lineage holders of the Karma Kagyu is known as the Golden Rosary of Kagyu Fathers. They are: Vajradhara (Tib. *Dorje-Chang*), Tilopa (989-1069 CE), Naropa (1016-1100 CE), Marpa (1012-1097 CE), Milarepa (1040-1123 CE), Gampopa (1079-1153 CE), Düsum Khyenpa, 1st Karmapa Lama (1110-1193 CE), Drogon Rechen (1148-1219 CE), Pomdrakpa (1170-1249 CE), Karma Pakshi, 2nd Karmapa Lama (1204-1283 CE), Orgyenpa (1230-1312 CE), Rangjung Dorje, 3rd Karmapa Lama (1284-1339 CE), Yungtön Dorjepel (1296-1376 CE), Rolpe Dorje, 4th Karmapa Lama (1340-1383), 2nd Shamarpa Khacho Wangpo (1350-1405 CE), Deshin Shekpa, 5th Karmapa Lama (1384-1415 CE), Ratnabhadra (dates unknown),Thongwa Dönden, 6th Karmapa Lama (1416-1453 CE), Jampal Zangpo (1427-1489 CE), Paljor Dondrup,

1st Goshir Gyaltsab (1427-1489 CE), Chödrak Gyatso, 7th Karmapa Lama (1454-1506 CE), 1st Sangye Nyenpa Rinpoche Tashi Paljor (1457-1525CE), Mikyö Dorje, 8th Karmapa Lama (1507-1554 CE),5th Shamar-pa Kongchok Yanglak (1526-1583CE), Wangchuk Dorje, 9th Karma-pa Lama (1555-1603CE), 6th Shamarpa Chokyi Wang-chuk (1584-1629 CE), Chöying Dorje, 10th Karmapa (1604-1674 CE), 7th Shamar-pa Yeshe Nyingpo (1631-1694 CE), Yeshe Dorje, 11th Karma-pa (1676-1702 CE), 8th Shamar-pa Chokyi Dondrup (1695-1732 CE, Changchub Dorje, 12th Karma-pa Lama (1703-1732 CE), 8th Tai Situpa Chokyi Jungney (1699-1774 CE), Dudul Dorje, 13th Karma-pa Lama (1733-1797 CE), 10th Shamar-pa Mipham Chodrub Gyatso (1742-1793 CE), 9th Situpa Pema Nyinche Wangpo (1774-1853 CE), Thekchok Dorje, 14th Karma-pa Lama (1798-1868 CE), Jamgon Kongtrul (1813-1899 CE), Khakyab Dorje, 15th Karma-pa Lama (1871-1922 CE), 11th Situpa Pema Wangchuk Gyalpo (1886-1953 CE), 2nd Jamgon Rinpoche Palden Khyentse Oser (1904-1953 CE), Rangjung Rigpe Dorje, 16th Karma-pa (1924-1981 CE), 12th Situpa Pema Tönyö Nyinje (1954—present CE) or 14th Shamar-pa Mipham Chokyi Lodro (1952—2014 CE), 17th Karma-pa Ogyen Trinley Dorje (1985—present) or 17th Karma-pa Trinley Thaye Dorje (1983—present).

2. Chos-sku tse' dGonpa, Khangsar

The household named Chos sku tse (*chos-sku-rtse*) is situated at the top of Khangsar village. Chos-sku tse'i dGonpa is considered to be one of the oldest Gonpas in Lahul. It is said that this monastery was built in the thirteenth or fourteenth century by a lama of the sTag-lung bKa'rgyud-pa school. There is also reference of this gonpa in the *Phugtal Bo-yig* of Zanskar of 1450 CE. The text reads as *'nyung-ti rgyal-po phul-ba'i. chos-sku tse gon-pa yan-mchod lam-khral zho-gling gye-mur tshun gre-mos bzhi-de lung-pa phu mdo dang bchas-pa phul'* which means 'The king of Kullu offered upto the monastery of Chos-sku-tse; the road tax from Zho-gling to Gemur, and offered the whole valley of gZhi(bzhi)-de. Gre-mos(?)'. In this text the geographical places of Chos-sku-tse, Zho-gling, Gemur and gZhi are well known villages in the Bhaga valley. Here the offerings made by the king of Kullu indicates that the upper part of Lahul, i.e. the Bhaga and Chandra valleys were under the domination of the Raja of Kullu. The incident occurred in around 1450 CE.

The old building is now in ruins and the traces of paintings can still be seen on one of the inner side walls of ruins. The present new building is not impressive and it looks like a local residential house (Pl. 41).

Pl. 41 : Side view of the Gonpa and the main altar

However, the clay and metal images and other ritual objects and ancient scriptures deserve special mention and have now been shifted to this newly constructed building (Pls.42-43). Among the clay images mention is made of Sakyamuni, Vajrasattva, Akshobhya, Avalokitesvara, Amitayus, Urgain-pa and a monk. Buddha Sakyamuni is seated in *dhyanamudra* and his right hand in *bhumisaprsamudra* and the left in the lap carrying the bowl while the image of Vajrasattva is shown seated in *dhyanamudra* holding *vajra* in his right and *ghanta* in the left hands with three pointed crowns. The image of four-armed Avalokitesvara is shown seated in *ardhaparyankasana* on a lotus pedestal with one of his right hands in *varadamudra* and a pair of hands in front of his breast holds *padma* and *mala* and the other hands are with a baton, flask and jewel. Akshobhya is shown in *dhyanamudra* on *padmasana* and has three pointed crowns on his head. The image of Amitayus is also shown seated in *padmasana* and holding a vase of life-giving ambrosis in his left hand while his right is in *bhumisaparsamudra*. But three pointed crown from his head is missing, perhaps damaged. These clay images are dated around the fifteenth century.

Pl. 42 : Clay image of Avalokitesvara; Akshobhya and Vajrasattva

Pl. 43 : Clay image of Urgyan-pa; Amitayus; and Monk

Another artefact which deserves mention is that of a brass or precious metal plaque *Ja-khyung*, depicting Buddha Amoghasiddhi seated on khyung (*bya-khyung, garuda*) and other metal images (Pl. 44). Chakrasamvara and Kalachakra Tantras are the main sources for the various lineages of Tantric Buddhist practice. Historically, Garuda is the king of birds. In Tantric Buddhism, Garuda is yet another form in which various Buddhas arise for the purpose of removing disease and injury caused by *nagas*. Various forms of Garuda are found in both the Nyingma and Sarma traditions.

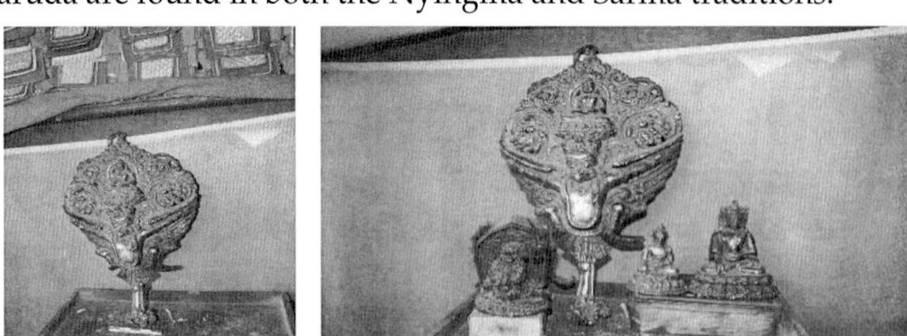

Pl. 44 : Ja-khyung and other metal images

The other metal images are that of seated Buddha and Akshobhya. Both the images are shown seated in *vajraparaynkasana* in *dhyanamudra.* Their right hands are shown in *bhumisaparsamudra* while the left hands placed on their laps (Pl. 45).

Pl. 45 : Buddha Sakyamuni and Akshobhya in bhumisaparasamudra

Another metal image in the collection is that of Vajradaka (*rdo-rje kha-dro*) a deity belonging to the larger category of the Chakrasamvara Cycle of Tantras (Pl. 46). He is shown in a seated position with the legs loosely arranged in front. He is shown with a radiant face, and his two hands at the heart performing the King of Desire *mudra,* holding a *vajra* on his right and a *ghanta* on his left. He has three eyes, hair flowing upward, and adorned with bones, jewels and the eight great *nagas*. He is wearing a lower garment of tiger skin, with the left leg extended.

Another important metal ritual object is that of the Mandala of Akshobhya. It is partly made of copper and partly in brass or mixed metal. At the center of the *mandala* is Buddha Akshobhya shown in seated position. The right hand is extended across the knee in *bhumisaparsa-mudra* while the left is placed in the lap in the *dhyanamudra.* With the legs folded in *vajrasana* above a moon disc and lotus seat and is surrounded by a nimbus of areola. The eight goddesses, each with one face and two hands occupy the surrounding circle are shown seated in relaxed posture. The floor of the palace *mandala* is square. The shape of the enclosure marks the extent of the palace walls with T- shaped structures at the four cardinal directions crowned with human figurines. Outer circles' are decorated with a ring of lotus petals and floral designs. This is a unique object not reported from other sites so far (Pl. 47).

Pl. 46 : Vajradaka (rdo-rje kha-dro)

Pl. 47 : Mandala of Akshobhya (mi drug pa'i kyi khor)

The eight goddesses, each with one face and two hands occupy the surrounding circle are shown seated in relaxed posture. The floor of the palace *mandala* is square. The shape of the enclosure marks the extent of the palace walls with T- shaped structures at the four cardinal directions crowned with human figurines. Outer circles' are decorated with a ring of lotus petals and floral designs. This is a unique object not reported from other sites so far.

3. Lha-khang, Khangsar Khar (Khang-gsar mkhar)

The Castle of village Khangsar is the residence of the Thakur family and waziri of Lahul under the British Government and Tak-tsang Repa stayed here for some time around 1615CE. The Khar is an impressive multi-stored structure inspired by hill architecture.

It is one of the largest and oldest heritage buildings in Lahul valley (Pl.48). The massive stone building possesses an amazing number of rooms and a large inner courtyard surrounded by tall wooden columns with fanciful, carved brackets. The atrium provides light for the adjoining chambers. It is said that the local people of the area contributed great labour in the construction and huge wooden beams and columns were brought from Mooling village and Meme Kasse of Jispa was the wood carver.

Pl. 48 : Khangsar Khar, side view; wooden decorations

The wooden beams and columns were beautifully carved. On the second floor is the dance hall, locally known as *Tshom-chhedmo* about 16m x 16m in dimension. The roof is supported by two thick and high wooden round columns in the middle of the floor. The roof of the *tshom-khang* or the floor of its upper floor is left open around these two wooden columns which allows light to come in from the sky. The upper floors and flat roofs are reached by means of wooden ladders at different locations.

The *chhod-khang* (*mchod-khan*) is located on the third floor which contains beautiful sacred images and a large collection of sacred books, including the Kan-gyur. A magical statue of Paldan Lhamo and a miraculous image of Mela-Repa are the main attraction of this shrine. It is believed that the image of Mela repa is now missing or no longer there. Tshe-bdag-mo, a goddess said to have been brought from Jispa is the Srungma, the guardian deity of Chhodpa. Manuscripts and other religious scriptures are stacked in old wooden bookshelves (Pl.49). Some arms and chain armour and a number of ancient round bucklers of rhinoceros hide, etc are preserved here.

Pl. 49 : Religious scriptures

The shrine is being maintained by the residents of sTod valley like an independent monastery and Lama-priest is deputed on rotation basis from Gemur monastery for the period of three years.

Annual festival called the festival of *Chhodpa* (*mchhod-pa*=Worship), an old folk tradtion, is held in the Khar (mKhar=palace) of the Thakurs of Khangsar, twice in a year in the summer and winter called *Yar-chhod (dbyar-mchhod=* Summer Worship) on 15th of 7th month and *Gun-chhod (dgunmchhod* = Winter Prayer) on the 15th of 2nd month of the Tibetan calendar. Lion dance is the main performance of the occasion and is the main attraction for the people. It is a festival for entertainment of the people and is connected with important seasonal agricultural operations. The mowing of grass and harvesting of crops starts immediately after the *Yar-chhod* and the operations connected with sowing starts sometime after the *Gun-chhod.* The play is enacted in a hall on the second floor called Tshom-chhedmo. The dancers dance between the walls and the four pillars. There also sit the spectators around. Some others sit on the upper floor who watch the show down through a wide opening in the upper floor.

4. dZong Gonpa, Tinno

The village is located on the north-east of Keylong at a distance of about 15 km on the left bank of Bhaga River, opposite to Kwaring village. It is said that earlier there were two monasteries, viz. dZong gonpa founded by Zong meme and Pala (Pa-la) gonpa by Pala meme. The ruined Pala gonpa is located slightly above the village on a ridge towards the south east, and is said to have been damaged from the avalanche. The ruined structures of four rooms and a passage in the middle are still visible at the site. dZong Gonpa lies above the village about a kilometer away towards north-east of the village in between the rocky cliff rising to a height of about 40metres (Pl.50). Water drips from the crevices of the rock and is collected below. It is told that when smoke is made below the rock the flow of the water increases. It is the only source of water here.

To reach the gonpa one has to climb through concrete stairs. It is said that earlier there were two storied structures but it crumbled down due to decay of some of the wooden pillars. It is now single storied. The small monastic complex, about rectangular fitted well between narrow passages within the rock cliff, is oblong in plan and facing north-west and consists of, as it comes on way, an independent rectangular structure followed by a mchod-rten and four other structures. The entry is through a wooden door jamb, though plain but the outer tier is decorated with diamond motif. On the lintel is an inscription in Bhoti scripts. The main shrine is an admixture of a cave—cum-structure with its back serving as a cave while the front being covered with raised walls from three sides.

Pl. 50 : Panoramic view of Zong Gonpa

This semi-apsidal structure is facing north-west and has a single door opening towards north-west. Its elevation shows a low raised platform over which are the walls supporting the flat roof. The whole structure is built of stones mixed with mud and husk mortar. The platform inside towards the north-east is hewn out of rock while that on the south-west is built of stones and plastered with clay. The two windows are on the north wall. The ceiling rests on wooden beams and rafters. The partly flat roof is supported by two wooden columns. The columns have a tapering torus followed by square shafts topped by floral abacus and double sided floral brackets.

Within the shrine on the central wall is the altar and the clay images of Avalokitesvara on the left, Padmasambhava in the center, mChod-rten and Mila-Repa on the right are accommodated within five alcoves partly covered with wooden frames. The other antiquarian remains are eleven-headed Avalokitesvara and Amitayus in brass; terracotta plaques depicting Padmasambhava with family tree, *mandala,* triangular plaque, a pair of cymbals, circular coiled stone lamp *(Gyam-mchhod),* lamps and *thang-kas* (Pls.51-52). Of the images, the smaller one of Padmasambhava is said to have been brought from Pala gonpa near the village.

Pl. 51 : Avalokitesvara, Padmasambhava, mChod-rten and Mila-Repa

Pl. 52 : Close view of antiquarian remains

The circular coiled stone lamp (*Gyam-mchhod* or *brgya-mchhod* = hundred worship lamps, actually 108) is a round circular flat stone slab of diameter of about one and half feet (Pl. 53). On it is carved concentric circles, ridges and drains alternately with one hundred and eight holes for lighting the worship lamps. Oil can be put in it at one place and it spreads uniformly to all the lamps itself.

Pl. 53 : Circular coiled stone lamp

There are incomplete old books containing prayers to the Guru like *Le'u bdunma* (Pl. 54). The title of one of the books reads: *na-ra-ga dong sprugs rnal-'byor gyi spyi-khrus*. The colophon at page number 27a reads: *rnal-'byor gyi spyi khrus na-raga dong sprugs 'gyod tshang gyi rgyalpo'I bshags-pa glang-po-che rang 'bog gi rgyud las khol dang phyung-p'o. a-u-rgyan gyi mkhanpo padma-'byung gnas dang. kha-che'i pandita bi-mala mi-tra dang. bod kyi lo tsava snyags dsnyan ku mara dang rm-rin-chen mchog gis bsgyur cing zhus te gtan la phab p-'o.*

Pl. 54 : Religious scriptures and wooden desks

Thus the book informs that the book was translated into Tibetan by four scholars: Padmasambhava, Vimala Mitra, Jnyan Kumar and Ma Rin-chhen Chhog. The work, however, does not name the title of the original work and the language from which it was translated.

Within the complex on the right side of the gonpa is the mChod-rten, square in plan and is built of dressed stones mortared and plastered with local clay. The other structures in the complex are devoid of any decorations and these are being used for the residential as well as for storing purposes. This gonpa is maintained by the local villagers. The dKon-gnyer, the lama priest, is being deputed from Gemur gonpa for a period of three years.

5. Thugdam Chosling (thugs-dam chos-gling), Dartse

The village Darcha or Dartse is located at an altitude of about 3,360 m from mean sea level at the junction of Yotche nullah and the Zangskar River. The two rivulets meet at this place with the main Bhaga River coming from different directions. It is 24 km away from Keylong, the District Headquarters, on Leh road where a camping ground is available. It is the northernmost permanent settlement in Himachal Pradesh along the Manali-Leh Highway and is the end-point of a popular trek beginning in Padum, Zanskar. This village is mentioned in the *Ladvags-rgyal-rab* under Singge-nam-rgyal (1600 CE) and in the Kullu Raja Bidhi Singh's decree in which it is spelt as Da-tse. Moorcroft visited this place in 1820 and calls it Darcha Sumdo. The monastery, locally known as Dartse gonpa, is located just above the village. The place was blessed by sTag-tshang Ras-pa who stayed in the area for some time.

The present structure of the monastery was built during the time of Tashi Tamphel, of sTagna Gonpa in about 1870-80. The present gonpa is a double storeyed structure, the ground floor is being used for the purposes of storage (Pl. 55). While in the upper floor there are three separate chambers. The chamber on the east side is the main Chod-khang or Lha-khang. The other chambers on the west are being used for the purpose of residence of Dartse lama. The *Chod-khang* is square on plan. The entry is from west through a small door. The flat roof ceiling is supported by four square wooden columns. The main altar is located in front of the east wall (Pls.56-58). The clay images enshrined in the altar include Buddha, Guru Padmasambhava, eleven headed Avalokitesvara, Manjusri, Mahakala, rDo-rje Leg-pa, Jagmen, Mila-Raspa, Vajrabhairava, etc. These images are kept in a wooden showcase besides other day to day ritual worship objects.

Pl. 55 : Old and renovated structure of the monastery; proposed new building

Pl. 56 : Interior view of the Gonpa

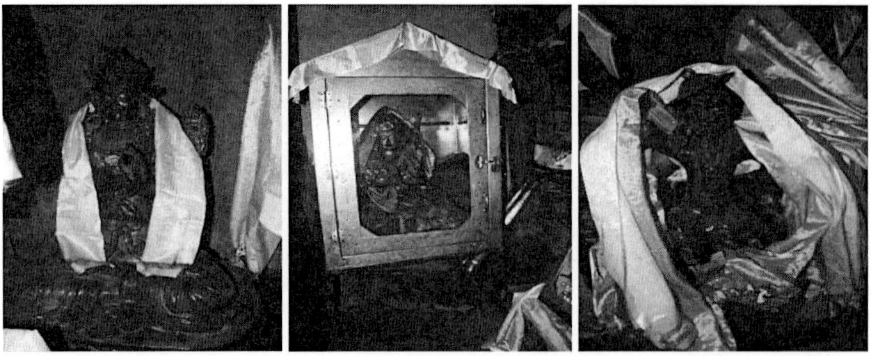

Pl. 57 : Maitreya; Padmasambhava; and rDo-rje Leg-pa

Pl. 58 : Padmasambhava; Avalokitesvara; and other deities

Thang-kas depicting Mithugpa, Tsepagmed are hanging on the walls and photos of Dalai Lama, sTag-tsang Rinpoche and Drug chhen Rinpoche are kept on the altar. The religious scriptures including a set of Kangyur are also stacked partly in wooden shelves on the north east corner and partly in steel shelves along the north wall. Butter lamps etc. has been kept in a separate west corner chamber (Pl. 59).

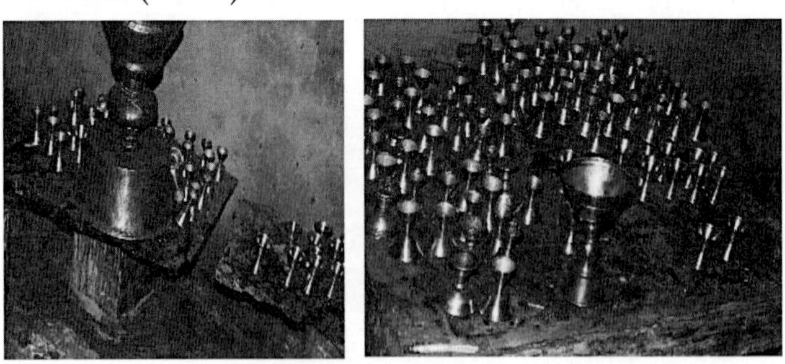

Pl. 59 : Butter lamps

There are 4-5 lamas. The main Lama is being deputed from Gemur gonpa on seniority as well as rotation basis for a period of three years. There is a proposal to shift the gonpa to a new building which is little above the present one and is under construction.

6. Photang (pho-brang), Jispa

The village of Jispa is situated at an elevation of 3,200 m from mean sea level and is located at a distance of 20 km north of Keylong and 7 km south of Darcha, along the Manali-Leh Highway. Jispa is one of the favorite places for an overnight stay while proceeding to Leh—Ladakh via Manali—Leh Highway. Moreover, the village is located right at the banks of River Bhaga.

Photang (*pho-brang*), a sacred structure was built in 1994 on the occasion of Kalachakra ceremony where HH Dalai Lama delivered Kalachakra sermons. The building is of two storeys, has a hall and arrangement of statues. There is a living room in the upper storey (Pl.60). There is a separate structure within the complex for the purpose of School which is now no longer in use.

Pl. 60 : Photrang, Jispa

The land where this grand structure was built was donated by Lama Rigzin of Kara-yogma. The lama-priest is sent here from Gemur monastery, each for one year term.

3 Other Religious Structures in sTod Valley

1. The Shrine dedicated to rDo-rje Leg-pa: It is located on the left side of the main Manali-Leh National Highway. This shrine is revered by all the villagers of the valley. rDo-rje leg-pa is a tutelary deity of the area and is one of the highest-ranking *'Jig rten pa'i srung ma*, tutelary deity of the common folk. In 1994, it was shifted to the present site at the instance of the HH Dalai Lama where a new chamber was built to house the deity (Pl. 61). Earlier it was placed in a small shrine under a huge juniper tree below the present national highway.

Pl. 61 : Shrine dedicated to rDo-rje Leg-pa, Jispa

The new shrine has a single chamber with sufficient space for circumambulation and is raised on a high platform. The deity is shown riding on a light brown hill-goat. He is in dark-red colour and has one face and three eyes with a gaping mouth. He wears a purple-brown hat. His right hand brandishes *vajra* while his left hand clutches a heart.

On the right side of this shrine is another chamber which is exclusively meant for burning lamps. Outside the fortified complex, *Mane-dhungyur* is kept in a separate chamber. On the road side, there is a Mane-wall with inscribed pebbles and slabs.

2. Yarzhi gonpa is located on the top of hillock on the left side of the Nallah above Yarzhi hemlet of the Jispa village. Approach to this shrine is through kaccha path about half an hour's walk from the village proper. This shrine was an important meditation center used by the local high ranking lamas from time to time. The ruined structures of the shrine revealed that originally it has double storeyed and it is said that the original construction was made by one elderly Meme Kasse of the village (Pl. 62). The present structure was raised very near to the ruined structure on the left side partly by using the materials from the old structure (Pl. 63). It is single storeyed with two chambers and open verandah over a high raised platform. The entry is from the south-east through stone stairs. The square chamber on the west is the shrine while on the east one is kept for day to day use. The roof of which is flat and rest on beams supported by a single wooden column. The side walls are of stones.

Pl. 62 : View of the old structure of Yarzi gonpa

Pl. 63 : Newly constructed Gonpa

The clay sculptures, *thankas* and other ritual objects retrieved from the old shrine are enshrined on the north wall in wooden glass showcases (Pls. 64-65). The main statues include Padmasambhava, Buddha, Tara, Maitreya, Manjusri, four-armed Sadaksari-Lokesvara, Vajrabhairava, metal rDor-rje and counch-shell, etc.

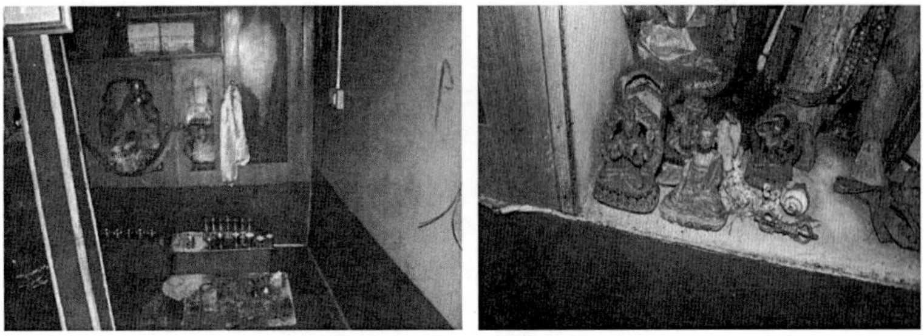

Pl. 64 : Main altar with clay image of Padmasambhava; Miniature clay images and other religious instuments

Pl. 65 : Buddha, Vajrabhairava; Manjusri and Sadakasari-Lokesvara

rDor-rje lag-pa is the main protector (*Srungma)* of the gonpa. The gonpa has a good collection of old *thangkas* but not in display. The metal vase and an inscribed stone slab are other objects. The metal vase is kept in a separe chamber along with butter lamps etc. while inscribed stone slab is found in the front of the small front court (Pl. 66).

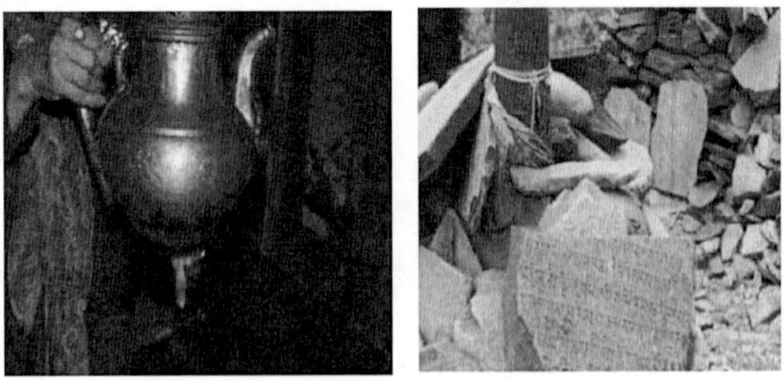

Pl. 66 : Metal Vase; inscribed stone slab

3. Buddhist Shrine at Pa-Lhamo: This site is located at an altitude of 3825 m above mean sea level and is situated at a distance of about four km from village Rarik and about 10 km from Darcha on Zanskar-Sumdo trek route. The construction of the pacca road on this track is in progress. The shrine is dedicated to goddess Paldan Lhamo and she resides there. While crossing the bridge over the Zanskar River one has to stop for a while and worship the goddess in a small shrine which is on the left bank of the river. On the other side of the river, there are two new shrines, one dedicated to goddess Paldan Lhamo and the other goddess Kali (Pls. 67-69).

Palden Lhamo (dPal-ldan lha-mo), the 'Glorious Goddess', is the main protective goddess of the valley. Palden Lhamo has one face and two arms. On the inner level of symbolism, she holds in her mouth the demon of mental afflictions. She is shown riding on a mule and holding a skull cup in her left hand. Around her waist is a belt hung with severed heads. Her red hair rising upward represents the blazing fire of perfect wisdom (*jnana*). She wears the five-skull crown showing that she has extinguished the five poisons (greed, anger, ignorance, pride, and jealousy). The third eye of wisdom is wide open in the middle of her forehead. The peacock-feather parasol of ultimate attainment rises above her head. A long necklace of fifty severed heads is strung on a wire representing intestines. The fifty heads correspond to the fifty worldly states of mind that must be cut off.

Pl. 67 : Shrine dedicated to goddess Paldan Lhamo

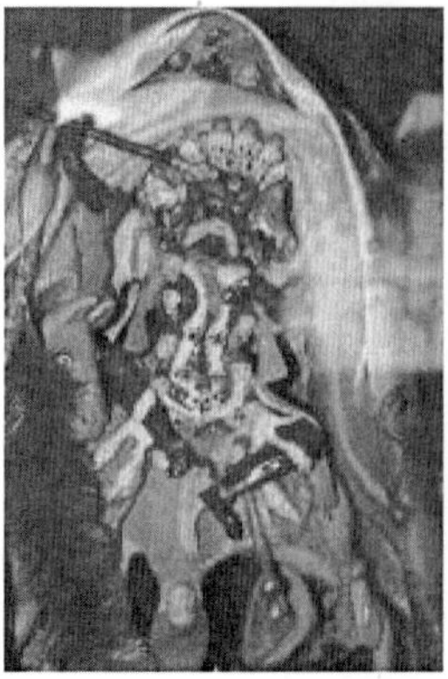

Pl. 68 : Newly built Shrine and image of Paldan Lhamo

Pl. 69 : Shrine dedicated to Kali

4. The Buddhist Rock Engravings and foot-imprint: In the sTod Valley, three rock engravings and inscribed boulders are found at Shangbhar village. These sacred engraved figures had a protective function for those passing in front of them. Of which, one huge boulder contains three images of Bodhisattva (Pl. 70), two images including the depiction of standing Bodhisattva Maitreya and other Bodhisattva on the south face while Bodhisattva is depicted on the north face. Maitreya has the flask above his shoulder. Both the hands of Maitreya is shown in front of the chest in *dharmacakramudra*. Three pointed crown is on his head. The Bodhisattva on the north face of the rock is also shown standing and wearing a three pointed crown on his head. His right hand is in *varadamudra* while his left hand in *vitarkamudra*.

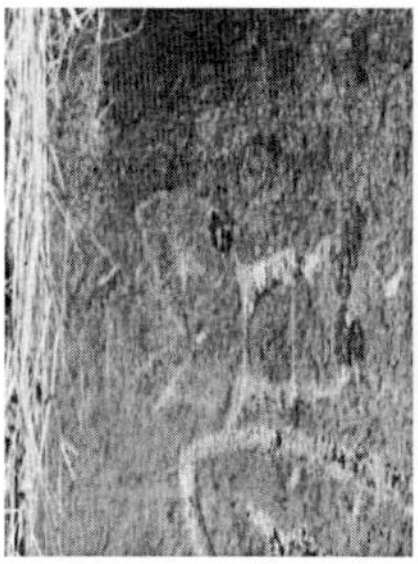

Pl. 70 : Maitreya and Bodhisattva on south face and Bodhisattva on north face

In another stone slab facing east, there is an image of Bodhisattva Manjusri engraved on it (Pl. 71). The image is shown in standing position and holding stem of the lotus in his left hand and sword on his right indicates that he is depicted here as an attendant of the historical Buddha. He is wearing a three pointed crown on his head. He is waring *dhoti* type garment and a long garland. In another triangular stone stele with the figure of *mchod rten* carved in low relief is kept on a boundary wall. In the centre of the cultivated field at Kolong, there is an image of Buddha engraved on a huge solid rock. The image is shown seated in *padmasana* and in *dhyanamudra* (Pl. 76). These engravings are the first traces of spread of Mahayana Buddhism in the valley and on stylistic ground these rock images are assigned a date in between seventh-eighth century to eleventh-twelfth centuries of the present era.

Pl. 71 : Standing image of Bodhisattva Padmapaniand stone stele with engraved mchod rten from Shrangbar

Pl. 72 : Buddha engraved on huge boulder, Kolong and Imprint of foot, Meh

A single huge imprint of the foot has been located on the left side of the ancient pathway linking the Meh or Mes village and Gemur Gonpa (Pl. 72). The imprint is highly venerated by the pilgrims during their enroute to Gemur Gonpa.

5. mChod-rtens and Mani-walls: The Buddhist Stupas are of three kinds, *saririka* Stupa raised over the relics of Buddha or Arhants. *Paribhogika* Stupas are the Stupas which enshrine the objects which have been used by the Buddha such as robe, bowl or walking staff. *Uddesika* Stupas were erected just for worshipping and contained no relics or to enshrine scriptures. The Vajrayana tradition attributes the components of the Stupa to each of the five elements (earth, water, fire, air and space). These elements represent the different stages in the transformation of psycho-spiritual energy in the path to enlightenment. Hence being an object for devotion, the Stupa also became an instrument for meditative visualisation.

However in the Tibetan Buddhist tradition eight type of stupas or mchod rtens (མཆོད་རྟེན་ཆ་བརྒྱད་, *mchod rten cha brgyad*) that are found in the Himalayan region which represent eight important events in the life of Buddha Sakyamuni. The term *mchod rten* means 'receptacle of worship'and its symbolism is multifaceted for the local communities, the monasteries and pilgrims for centuries. These are constructed according to specific measurements laid down in *stūpa* manuals or treatises (*mchod rten thig rtsa*) and emphasis has to be put on the filling of the cavities, in summary consisting of relics, *dhāraṇīs*, *maṇḍalas* and their respective offerings followed by a special consecration ritual (*pratiṣṭhā*: *rab gnas*) transforming religious and sacred or holy objects. *mChod rtens* are in a variety of sizes, shapes and styles. Some are monumental and have a huge presence in the landscape. Some are confined within the walls of a monastery, and house the relics of famous lamas but in due course they came to be regarded as holy symbols and were built empty as mere memorials of the dead, whether the dead be some well-known saint or some local landowner. Other small ones are within personal shrines, or are painted on walls or ceilings. Large poles with prayer-flags with prayers are fixed in the centre of the earlier *mChod rtens.* The *mchod rten* is a nearly solid edifice, built in the form of a large square base in several sections, on which is placed the larger half of an inverted dome decorated with a lotus cornice crowned by a square *harmikā* and tapering pillar of wood with a series of 13 wheels or rings carved with horizontal grooves surmounted by a crescent-moon, sun-disc and jewel. The eight type of *mchod rtens* generally found in the Buddhist Himalaya region are:

1. *The Lotus Blossom Stupa of the Buddha's Birth* (*sku bltams mchod rten* symbolizes the birth of Siddhartha, in the sixth century BCE. The steps of the stupa are round and decorated with lotus petals.
2. *The Enlightenment Stupa (byang chub mchod rten)* symbolizes the attainments of enlightenment after sitting in meditation for 49 days under a tree at Bodhgaya. The steps of the stupa are rectangular and undecorated.
3. *The Stupa of Turning the Wheel of Dharma (cho 'khor mchod rten)* represents the point at which the Buddha began to 'turn the wheel of the Dharma', to teach the path to enlightenment to others. Also known as the Stupa of Many Doorways, the steps are adorned with doorways symbolising the opening of the doors of the Dharma.
4. *The Great Miracle Stupa (cho 'phrul gyi mchod rten)* commemorates the Buddha's display of miracles at Sravasti. Each of the four steps, in each of the four directions have central extensions.
5. *The Stupa of the Descent from Tushita Heaven (lha bab mchod rten)* represents the Buddha's return from the celestial realms in

order to continue teaching the people. Each side of the *mchod rten* has a stairway in the centre of the four steps.

6. *The Stupa of Reconciliation* (*dbyen bsdum mchod rten*) symbolizes the Buddha's reuniting of his monastic followers after they had become divided by disagreement. The steps are octagonal with eight corners and eight sides.
7. *The Victorious Stupa (rnam rgyal mchod rten)* symbolizes the Buddha's agreement to extend his life by three months, after one of his followers had pleaded with him not to pass away. The steps of the stupa are round.
8. *The Parinirvana Stupa (myang 'das mchod rten)* marks the Buddha's passing into *nirvana,* a state of true peace which is beyond death. There are no steps in this stupa, the vase rests directly on the throne.

Similarly, *Mani*-wall is used to designate walls of about three to four feet in height and four to eight feet in breadth, but their length varies. These *mani*-stones are usually placed along the ancient paths or routes or roadsides and rivers, a form of devotional *cintamani.* Rough, irregularly rectangular stone slabs in sizes, and bearing inscriptions in Bhoti or *Lantsa* characters, or adorned with images of deities, lean against the upper part of the wall or are laid down on the top. Some of the large *Manis* have a *mchod rten* at both their ends. The most frequent inscription met with in the stone slabs is the six-syllabic prayer: *Om mani padme hum*; or adorations of Vajrasattva, *Om, ah, hum vajra guru padma siddhi hum*; of Vajrapani, *Om Vajrapani hum*; or mystical ejaculations, *Om, ah, hum,* etc. Sometimes the names of deities, Sakyamuni, Padmapani, Padmasambhava, Vajrapani and different recluse are engraved on the stone slabs. Large poles with prayer-flags with prayers are fixed in the centre of the earlier *mChod rtens* and at places these poles are attached at the ends. The slabs are votive offerings made for the purpose of obtaining the fulfilment of particular wishes and the travelers while passing along these *Mani*-walls leave them on the left hand in order to follow the succession of the letters of the inscriptions.

There are numerous Buddhist *mchod rtens* and *mani*-walls scattered along the roads or pathways or near the villages in Tod valley. At some locations these have already been included with the religious edifices. While exploring the area in question, the authors discovered on the right bank of the Bhaga River for the first time a petroglyphic site, locally known as Mangalak where a variety of *mchod rten* types have also been found engraved on a huge rock face (Pls.73-74).

Pl. 73 : Petroglyphs of the rock face at Mangalak

Pl. 74 : Types of mchod rtens engraved on rock at Mangalak

Karing ruins are located on a level ground above the village Kwaring. On its north-western corner just behind the modern double-storeyed house belonging to the Karing Khar is located the ruins of an old structure which was perhaps the ancient palace or Khar of the local chieftain. The ruined structures comprises a number of interconnected chambers and are built of small dressed stones mortared with clay mixed with straw etc. A few distance away from this ruined structures are a huge *Mane*-wall measuring about 8.50 m x 2.50 m x 1.75m and built of random rubble masonry without binding materials (Pl. 75). Over it are placed innumerable inscribed stone pieces and slabs. Over and above these inscribed stone pieces on both the corners are placed two beautifully carved and finely finished blocks of stone base of a pillar or base of the wooden pinnacle of the mchod-rten measuring 10x10x6 inches, a unique piece of architectural member which indicates that there could have been a beautiful building or structure mostly of stone. Such types of finished architectural members have not been reported so far from this region.

Pl. 75 : Mani-wall over which are inscribed stone slabs, pebbles and twin pillar bases and wooden parasol

Besides the above, village is dotted with number of mchod rtens and mani-walls at different locations in the village (Pl. 76). Of which two and a *mani*-wall are located at Ghantse, two along with mani-wall below Jabze and two mchod rtens have been found above Pangrong gonma. One mani-wall containing inscribed stone slabs has been found at in between Pangrong and Khulagmur.

Pl. 76 : mani-walls at different locations in the Karing village

Four *mchod-rtens*, one *pur-khang* (*spur-khang*) and one *mani*-wall have been located at village Rangrik. Of which the *pur-khang* has been built in the memory of Venerable Lama Ngag-dbang Thinley (1909-2000), the former Head Lama of Gemur Gonpa who expired on 18th December, 2000. While the other *mchod rten* was built by him in the memory of his son sometimes in the late sixties or early seventies of the twentieth century. It has recently been given a facelift by the family members (Pl.77).

Just below these edifices, there is another *mchod rten* near the site known as Rangrik-tsurma which appears to be built in the early nineteenth century. Fourth *mchod rten* is built in recent years in the memory of Lama Dundup of Khanthalpa by his sons.

Pl. 77 : Pul-Khang and mchod rten at Rangrik

In the hill-top above the village Keylad, a tower-like structure built of undressed stones can still be seen in ruined condition. In village Keylad four *mchod-rtens* have been located, of which two in row are erected in stones without mortar and in the center wooden pole had been fixed for flags. Both these *mchod rtens* are unique and not found elsewhere in the area which seems to be of early age (Pl. 78). Presently both are in dilapidated conditions and need urgent repairing. The small one is located in the center of the village and it is raised on a simple platform while the fourth one is of recent years (Pl. 79).

Pl. 78 : mChod rtens from Keylad

Pl. 79 : mChod rtens at Keylad

At village Sarang, a long *mani*-wall with inscribed stone slabs and boulders and a *mchod-rten* was located in its outskirts (Pl. 80). Sarang is also mentioned in the votive documents of the time of Kullu king Pratap Singh (1539-84 CE) and similar documents of the time of Prabat Singh (1584-1618 CE). Repairs to the mchod rten have already been initiated by the local inhabitants. Another site locally known by the name, Tsa-ti, is located in between Sarang and Keylad villages. There is a mani-wall containing inscribed stone boulders (Pl. 81).

Pl. 80 : Mani-walls and mchod rten from Sarang

Pl. 81 : Mani-wall from Tsati

In the vicinity of village Kolong, there are numerous *mchod-rtens* and *mani*-walls. One of the passage or gateway type mchod rten, locally known as Mani Zungthen near Kolong village attracts the attention of every passerby. It marks the approach to the settlement locally known as Khangsar. It is unique and uncommon from the smaller, simpler ones in Lahuli style (Pls. 82-83).

Pl. 82 : Two mchod rtens and Mani-wall at Zungthen

The stone built *mchod rten* is composed of a square base on which lie three receding crossed shaped steps decreasing in height. There are three openings in each step according to the model of *mchod rten*. A high circular dome tops the structure. Each element of the *mchod rten* is separated from the other by projecting slabs. The passage in the plinth is roofed with wooden beams. Below the *mchod rten* within each wall of the passage there is a niche marking the location of a now gone statue. The inner space is composed of four side walls covered by a wooden lantern ceiling. The wooden *Chhattra* is missing from the top and is now kept in the empty, undecorated dome of the gateway. The elaborate double-staircase form with unusual small openings is a unique form and seems to be original, but is uncommon in this area. The exterior face is now plastered with cement. This form is broadly reminiscent of a Western Tibetan *mchod rten* and dated to eleventh-twelfth century CE.

Pl. 83 : Close view of the passage or gateway type mchod rten at Mani Zungthen

Just near to this gateway type mchod rten, there is another mchod rten which is located on the right side of the main road connecting Kolong and Khangsar. It was built sometime in the end of the twentieth century. Another mchod rten is located near the old house of Pankarpa. Three mchod rtens have been found in the center of the agriculture field near the house of Yarongpa which appears to be of early date(Pl. 84). These three mchod rtens are of different styles and shapes and built of stone slabs without mortar. Presently these edifices are not in a sound condition and need immediate attention for their restorations. Few meters away from this site on the ancient pathway and very near to Government School, there is another mchod rten with a mani-wall (Pl. 85).

Pl. 84 : Three mchod rtens near Yarongpa household

Pl. 85 : mchod rten and Mani-wall near Govt. School, Kolang

On the left side of Shiti-nallah on the old pathway locally known as Kolongdum, there are two *mchod rtens* and a *mani*-wall (Pl. 86). Both the *mchod rtens* have recently been repaired by using modern materials but are in dilapidated condition.

Pl. 86 : Two mchod rtens and Mani-walls at Kolongdum

Two mchod rtens with inscribed stone slabs are located on the outskirts of village Meh on the left side of the old pathway leading to Gemur Gonpa, both are in good state of preservation (Pl.87). Three modern mchod rtens and two mani-walls have been located within the village.

Pl. 87 : Two mchod rtens and inscribed stone slabs on the outskirts of Meh village

Apart from Zong Gonpa in Tino village, there are numerous *mChod-rtens* and *mane*-walls scattered here and there in the fields (Pl. 88).

Pl. 88 : mChod-rtens and mane-walls within the village fields

Just below the present Chuku tsi Gonpa at Khangsar, there are two mchod rtens which were erected earlier and contemporary with the original gonpa. Both are built on a solid rock. The materials used are rough stones and the outer surfaces are plastered with mud mortar (Pl. 89).

Pl. 89 : Twine mchod rtens, Chukutsi

Both are of Enlightenment type of *mchod rtens* comprising of flight of four steps which are perfectly square in shape and are free from embellishments and upon it stands the 'vase-shaped dome topped by the *harmika*-base and the *harmika* followed by a tier of thirteen wheels in the shape of thirteen disks or rings that taper off in height and circumference towards the top most wheel. All the wheels are of equal height and upon which is the moon in the shape of a crescent, and the radius of sun. These types of *mchod rtens* are most commonly found in the Lahul Valley. Here the top portion of one of the *mchod rten* is found missing, perhaps collapsed in due course. The present conditions of both the *mchod rtens* are in dilapidated conditions.

Three large sized *mchod-rtens* have been located at Shrangbar and a *mane*-wall containing inscribed stone slabs and boulders is found in between two *mchod rtens* (Pls. 90-91). One of the cylindrical boulder contains inscriptions in Tibetan characters the contents of which is yet to be deciphered. It appears that these *mchod rtens* were renovated earlier by using modern materials. The present conditions of these are in a deplorable conditions.

Pl. 90 : mChod rten; Mani-wall in between two mchod rtens

Pl. 91 : Mani-wall with inscribed stones

There were remnants of an ancient watch tower, known as Dankhar, the walls of which are of stone and wood at the edge of the plane overlooking the whole valley. Now this historical structure has completely been razed to the ground and a new building has come up.

Another site, locally known by the name Memepusha is not far from the village. Four *mchod rtens* are located here. Of which one on the south without parasol is said to have been built sometime in the later part of the twentieth century. While the other three are of earlier period (Pl. 92).

Besides the Lha-khang within the Khangsar Khar, there is a group of four *mChod-rtens* with mane-wall on the north-east corner said to be built in the memory of the former rulers (Pls.93-94). One gateway type of mchod rten has been located just on the back of the Khar-complex and one of the opening is now closed.

Pl. 92 : mChod rtens in row at Memepusha

Pl. 93 : Row of four mchod rtens in dilapidated conditions, Khangsar Khar

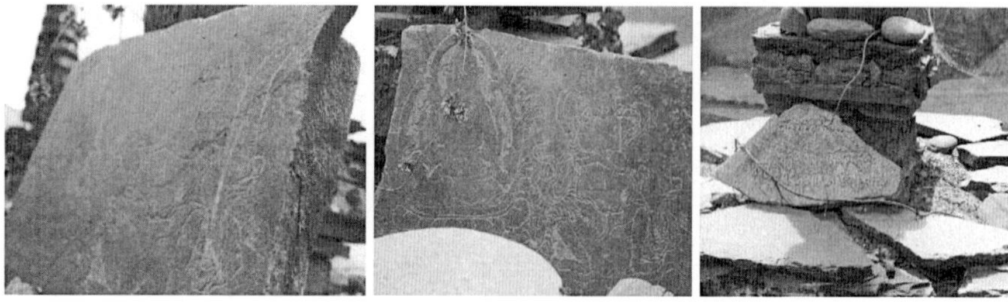

Pl. 94 : Carved stone slabs on above mchod rtens, Khangsar khar

It is said that earlier people used to go through the gateway but now it is found blocked due to construction of a new road. These *mchod rtens* are now in pathetic conditions and these historical remains are to be conserved for posterity.

In Jispa village, numerous other religious structures in the form of *mchod-rtens* and inscribed *mani*-walls have been located at various locations in the village.Some of which are of recent periods (Pl. 95).

Pl. 95 : Mane-walls and mChod rtens within the Jispa village

Two *mchod rtens* and one *mani*-wall have been located in the vicinity of village Gemur on the either side respectively of the present road. Of which it is said that the *mchod rtens* were built by the local erstwhile rulers as a memorial of their forefathers during the last century. One *mchod rten* and partly damaged *mani*-wall has been located on the left side of the road near village Bog and a few meters away from this place on the left side of the road is another long *mani*-wall (Pls. 96-97). The largest hitherto known *Mani*-wall is the Mani Ringmo which is situated on the right side of the present national highway leading to Jispa (Pl. 98). It is in deplorable conditions and need immediate repairing.

Pl. 96 : mChod rten and mani-wall,Bog

Pl. 97 : Mani-wall near Bog

Pl. 98 : Mani-wall, Maneringmo

Three *mChod rtens* and *mani*-wall have been located in the village of Darcha (Pl. 99). Of which two are found in good state of preservation. Third one with partly damaged *mani*-wall is just a little away from the village which appears to be of an earlier date. In the village Darcha —Sumdo, huge *mchod rten* has been built in recent times and is well maintained (Pl.100).

Pl. 99 : mChod rtens and mani-wall, Darcha

Pl. 100 : mChod rten, Darcha Sumdo

4 Historical Rock Inscriptions from sTod Valley

AH Francke located numerous inscriptions engraved on rocks, boulders and stone slabs from various sites from Lahaul valley and these were copied and published by him under the title *'Second Collection of Historical Inscriptions on Rocks and Stones from Western Tibet,* 1907'. These rock inscriptions were transiletrated and translated by the authors some times before and later published in the book entitled *'Historical Documents from Western Trans-Himalaya Lahul, Zanskar and Ladakh in* 1996'. Of which a few historical rock inscriptions relate to sTod region. However, the original texts of the rock inscriptions are at **Annexure III.** During our recent field works in the valley, efforts have been made to identify the exact locations of these sites of rock inscriptions, so far the authors could not locate the sites of these historical records.

B.127 Inscription in rock from Hayar, Tshewang rNamgyal and the king of Kullu Parbat Singh, A.D. 1700-1730

Transliteration

Om sua ta sta tya ma.

dge la zong srong byung ba'i grangs la ska nng nas no bla btsun steng zhal gnyis hyar jo rje bza mi gnyis, kyen la drangs.

Translation

Obeisance to the siddhas Happiness. Younger brother bla btsun, the husband along with his wife, the noble of the house of Hayar, the lord, wife and husband, were drawn up.

B.128 Votive inscription in Bhoti script from mChod rten at Kolong 1700-1730

Transliteration

Om svasti siddham. bla ma dang rje btsun jam pa'i dbyangs la phyag 'tshal lo sku gsum6 mingon du gyur ba'i ston pasangs rgyas dang. bsde snod gsum" gyis phyug pa'i dam chhos dang. Slab pa gsum'e gyis mdses pa i deg dun sde, skyabs gnas dkon mchhog gsum la gus phyag Islhal. Ae ma ho, "bka' rgyud rdo rje chhang chhen ti li na ro dang. mar pa mila sgam po (rgam po) thar sab pa. gnas phug pa dang Ipal pdan 'bnug pa'i zhabs. bka' rgyud bla ma rnams la phyag tshal lo." Ae ma ho.

physi snod kyi 'jig rten brgya gram rlung gyis stegs (brya brgya brlung gi steg). nang bchud Ayi sems chan od gsal Iha nas chhad, dgung sngon dbyibs lags baidu rya 'dra'i 'og. dog sa bkod egs padma dab brgyad steng, ga'u?' kha bsbyor gnam sa gnyis kyi bar. dgra bchom bzhugs gnas gangs dkar clang. mingos grub chhag khyil ma pang y-yu mtsho'i nub, ni rgyud ma chhad gnas nch dril bu ri. rgyal bas lung bstan ri bo gan dha la. dpa' bo dpa' mo'i 'du gnas ngo mtshar yul la g-yang chhags gar zha mkha gro'i gling. pho brang chhen po rgyal sa ma gar sang e alar yas (brjal ye) khang 'dra'i sku (skum) mkhar rtse (brtse) mo na. Lha sras chhos rgyal basng-gklhong la bstod. de dra'i mnga' o'g gar bya mkha' 'gro' i gling. sa la 'bur du mtho bu Sng stod Khangsar sku mkhar 'dir, mi dbang tshe dbang ('ang) rnam rgyal dbu rmog mtho us. Khyed kyi chhab srid bzang po'i sku mkhar ka (ska) ring 'dir gdung rgyud khyad phags od ysal Tha nas chhad yon gyi bdag po no no bsod nams dbang po dang sbyin bdao gtso (brtso) mo yum me tshe dbang rgyal mo yum sras gnyis kyis kyang. sku bde bar bskyong ba grogs dang yab kyi dgongs pa dsogs (rdsog) phyir du. gsung gi rten (brten) du je btsun mgur bum dang mam thar gchod pa ma bu gling mdsa chhos skyid bzhengs. sku'i rten (brten) du sprul sku'i zhing khams rje btsun gyi zhing khams. bla ma mchhod (chhod) pa'i dkyil thang, thugs kyi ten du byang chhub mchhod rten (brten). de sogs thugs dgongs rnam par dag pa i mdsad pa shin tu ngo mtshar chhe kye (skye) lags gsung rab di phyir dge dogs mdsad pai grangs. rkang thung ngos la dab bya du ba am sbrang btsi'i ro la bong ba khor ba Itar. nyal gro'irgyun bzhin bdud rtsi'i chhar Itar bab. khong g" zhal ngo grag zhan mams kyis kyang. phyogs nas lags par steg pa ngo mtshar chhe kye lags.

kye lang mkhar nas rgyal po bde jam rgyal mo nang gha dpal mo. rgyal mo dsom gzhan yang khang sar mkhar nas ga ga tshe dbang mam rgyal no mo tshe ring dsom ba steng zhal gnyis. steng khang nas ga ga no mo byor skyid steng zhal gnyis bar bog mkhar (khar)?" nas no kun bzang Ide rdo je sgol ma yab sras gnyis. smas kyi dgon pa nas a ne slab tsun ma. sa rang nas me me blo gros dpal mo steng zhal gnyis. ka (ska) nng nang nas thugs sras nomo gangs sman. a zhang dkun dga (kun gha) mas smad me me tshul khrims rgyal mtshan. gyen lad gong (gon) nas bsod nams (so nam) sing tsam me bza mi gnyis. ha yar nas rdo je bzang mo bza mi gnyÀs. chhe ling a chhe no mo skyid. rgyal sras bsod nams dpal bar no mo byor steng zhal gnyis. chhos rje jam dbyangs dkar po'i drung nas bka' drin chhe. shi la'i mkhar nas rgyal po tshe ring dpal de jo jo nadren steng zhal (zhal yas) gnyis kyi shin tu bka' drin chhe (stengzhal gnyis. shila nas a ma jo cho tshe ring sgrol ma khang sar nas a ma bag ma tshe dbang skyid).

Translation

Om, obeisance to the teachers. Obeisance to the teacher and the exalted Manjughosh. The Buddha who manifests himself in three forms; the excellent doctrine enriched by the three baskets, the organization, adorned by three kinds of teachings, I go to the refuge of the three precious ones - the object of refuge. Ae ma ho! I pay obeisance to the teachers of the lineage of the Ka-gyud sect: the great Vajradhara (the Adi- Buddha of the sect). Tilipad (tenth century A.D.), Naropad (956-1040), Marpa (1012-1097), Mila Repa (1052-1135), Gampopa (1079-1161), Tharsabpa, Nephugp and Paldan Dugpa. Ae ma ho! From outside the world is supported by air. The inner world (living beings) descended from the god Abhasvara. The blue sky'above appears like *vaidurya* and the earth below like eight petalled lotus, and the whole shape represents an amulet box (*ga'u*) which has a lid, base and large space in between. In the western direction of the white snowy mountain Tise (Kailash), the abode of Arhats, and the self-created turquoise like Lake Mapang (Mansarovar), lies the great holy place of Dilbu, situated on the unbroken chain of mountains. Here also lies the Gandhola Mountain, the holy place, prophesied by the.*Jinas* (Buddhas). This is a miraculous place where the heroes (guardian gods) and heroines (*dakinis*) meet, Lahul, the land of *dakinis,* is blessed in his manner. Reverence to the virtuous divine son, Parbat Singh, who resides at Magarsa, in the castle which is like a godly mansion. Lahul, the land of *Dakini,* is under the sway of such a king. Tshewang Namgyal, the lord of men, the worthy ruler, resides in a castle which is like a prominent engraving on the earth, at Khangsar, in sTod valley. Under his excellent rule, resides here in a castle at Karing, where the ten virtues have assembled, and the family (of Jos) whose progressive lineage has descended from the god Odsal (Abhasvara). Patron, Nono Sonam Wangpo and the chief patroness mother Tshewang Gyalmo, both mother and son, for fulfilling the wishes of the father, who was a companion and had given protection to the two, raised: for the holder of precepts a copy of Gurbum (the hundred thousand songs) of Jetsun Mila Repa and his biography, the two like mother and son, and autobiography of Lingza Chhoskyid; for the holder of body, *thangka* painting of Amitabha and Mila Repa; and the mandala of Lamas' Worship, and for the holder of the heart, Bodhisattva chaitya. Deeds of pure thoughts like those were wonderful. Kye legs!

The followers assembled for hearing the sermons on the excellent precepts and supporting the virtuous acts, numbered as if birds had gathered on a green tree or insects collected over the remains of honey drops. They came like the river or rain of ambrosia. His fame and praises spread wonderfully in the various directions. From Kyelang Khar came king Dejam, Queen Nangha Palmo and Gyalmo Zom. Moreover, from Khangsar Khar came elder brother Tshewang Namgyal, younger sister, Tshering Zompa, husband and wife. From Tengkhang, brother and younger sister Jorkyid, husband and wife. From Barbog Khar younger brother Kunzang De Dorje and Dolma, father and daughter, two. From the monastery of sMes came aunt La-btsunma (perhaps a nun); from Sarang, grandfather Lodee and Palmo, husband and wife; from Karing Nang, honourable younger sister Gangmen, and uncle Kunga, mother and son and grandfather Tshulkhrims Gyaltshan; from Kyelad Gong Sonam Singtsham, wife and husband, two, from Hayar, Dorje Zangmo, wife and husband, two; from Chheling elder sister and younger sister Kyid, and prince Sonam Palbar and younger sister Jor, husband and wife, two; virtuous king Jamyang Karpo has done great mercy by his presence; from Shila Khar Tshering Palde, elder brother, husband and wife, the two have done great mercy. (Husband and wife. From Shila came mother Tshering Dolma; from Khangsar mother Tshewang Kyid.)

B.135 Inscription on a mani at Khangsar

Transliteration

Rgyal sa

sur stan spur. rgyal sras dam pa spri tim sing

gi dbu mog tho zhing (dri) chhab srid rgyas 'gyur chig.

Translation

Good prince Pritam Singh, whose capital is situated at Sultanpur, may his crown be held high and the kingdom flourishing.

B.140 Votive inscription from village Bog, 18th -19th Century

Transliteration

Ae ma ho, gnas chhen khyad (khang) 'phags gar sha mkha' gro'i (mkhro'i) gnas. rdo rje gdan (rje.) tshungs ri bo gan dha la. ya mtshan smad byung dpal gyi dnil bu'i ri. sangs rgyas mams kyis byin gyis brlabs pa'i gnas. gangs ri dkar po dkar ti rtsi 'dra. ri gsum 'dus pa gnas chhen lab phyi dra, chhu gsum 'dus pa dpal gyi chhu bar dra. thams chad tshang ba rtsa ra rtsa gong 'dra. gnam la bltas na khor lo rtsibs brgyad dra. sa la blts na padma dab brgyad dra. log la bltas na bkra shis stags brgyad 'dra. Pho skyes tham chad dpa bo'i chha byad (bro ba'i chha byang) 'dra mo (ma) skyes tham chad khro mo chha byad (khro 'i cha dyad) 'dra. Skad rigs mi gchig (-) lo thsa tshogs pa 'dra. Yul lugs mi dra rgya bod dres pa 'dra chha lugs mi 'dra byis pa'i rgyan chha'dra.

Phu Na gnas bdag (dong khang) lha mo rang byon (-) bzhugs bar na rang byon thug rje chhenpo bzhugs. Mdo (de) Ru yi dam do phag mo bzhugs. Pho brang po sur tan puri yi rgyal po chhenpo bhir khyim senge'i dbu rmog mtho (tho) ba'i dus yul la dyangs chhag gar sha mkha'gro gling mi dbang pho brang. Khyad par khang sar nal dhar ma seng ge yum sras dbu rmog mtho zhing chhab srid dar ba'i dus. Dge bchu'I mkhrims kyi' khor 'bangs' dumdsad. Sdig bchu gtan nas. Brlag ba'i dpa' bo'i mchho. De'i mnga' og 'bog gi yul (gyul) mchhog na yon gi bdag po 'brug rgya mtsho dang. Yon gyi bdag m organ 'dso gnyis. De'i sras bkra shis bsam byeïrdang no no 'brug tshe dbang gnyis kyi btsun mo bstan 'dsin bu khrid dang no no a nu gnyis. Yang sras bstan' dsin tshe dbang dang Padma bu khrid gnyis.

Nang tshang tham chad dge ba 'i bsam pa chan. Dge ba'i las la 'bras buï.b'o. sngon tshe bsod nams bsags pa 'i mthu stobs las. Tshe dirï.pyod mi zad char bab ching. Phyi ma 'i don du dge ba dpag med mdsad. Khyad par yig drug stong ra chan gchig dang brgya gchig bzhengs. Mar gyud mtha med gro ba yoï. Sa gyi don du ldag bsam rnam par dag pa 'i mgo nas mdsad pa ngo mtshar chhe chhe.

Translation

Lahul, well developed land of the fairies and a great holy place—here are located the monastery of Gandhola resembling *Vajrasana* (Bodhgaya) and the miraculous and wonderful mount Drilbu. The holy place is blessed by all the Buddha's. Its white snowy mountains resemble the mount Tise. The three mountain ranges converging here resemble the holy place of Lab chhi, the three rivers confluence here resemble the great holy river Ganges. Thus fulfilling all sins like Tsari Tsegong. If one looks towards the sky it appears like the eight spoked wheel, if one looks upon the earth, it appears like eight petalled lotus, if one looks on the sides it appears like eight lucky signs. All men possess characters of heroes and all women that of Brikuti. People talking in unmatching tongues appear like the assembly of interpreters. The land of curious customs indicates the fusion of Indian and Tibetan culture. Bizarre apparels give the appearance of children's ornaments.

At the head of the valley resides the goddess of the holy places, self-born Lhamo. In the middle resides the All-merciful, Avalokitesvara and at the end of the valley resides the tutelary deity Vajravarahi. Great king Bikram Singh (1806-1816 CE), whose castle is situated at Sultanpur, his crown is held high. In well-developed Lahul, the land of *dakinis*, especially Khangsar. Here resides Dharam Singh, mother and son, his crown is held high and the kingdom is progressing. He rules his attendants and subjects with the law of ten virtues.

He who has conquered the ten sins, the excellent hero, under his sway lies the excellent village of Bog. Here the benefactor Dug Gyamtsho and benefactress Ganzom, the two, their son Tashi Sam... and younger brother Dug Tshewang, two and Tanzin Buthid, wife of the two, and younger sister Ami, two, and grandson Tanzin Tshewang and Padma Buthid, two. All the family members, well-wishers, in the tasks of welfare...with the strength of merits amazed in the former lives, here in this life...undiminishing rainfall ofî.. Unlimited virtuous deeds were done for the benefit in the next life. Especially the six syllable *mantra* was inscribed one thousand and one hundred times...innumerable living beings... for the benefit of...

B.141 Votive Inscription on Mani stone, Bog, referring Dharam Singh, (1770-1810) (Bhoti language and script)

Transliteration

... la rgyan. thuys rje spyan gyis (gyi)' gro la gzigs. mgon po spyan ras gzigs la phyag 'tshal lo. ae ma ho. de nas gangs (gang) ti si'i klung (glung) gi lho phyogs (phyog) su. sa gzhil la..byin chhags Iho'i dsam bu gling seng ge kha bab.

..bi khim (byi ma) seng ge dbu rmog mtho (tho) ba'i dus. yul la dyangs chhags sku mkhar (khar) khang sar rtser: mi dbang chhen po dharam seng ge'i dbu rmog mtho (tho) be 'i dus. Yul la dge behu mdsoms ba bog dir. mig gis khung brtsun rgyn shing pa'i rgyud lhun 'grub..'i mchhog gyur tshe dbang (dgyangs)chhos kyid dang a ma bsod (so) nams dang. a cho dngos brub dang no don. drub dang. nomo bzang mo dang.dpon chhen phags pa chhos phel dang. chhos byor dang, rdo rje hr'i kyab dang lag shes tshe dya..ma gan dsom dang. bu'i mchhog gyur tshe dbangs (dbyangs) bstan dsin dang tsha mo'i mchhog ygyur padma bu srid dang dge rtsi la sang ma sol ja bag sha rtsi don sing a rag byung. tshe dbang (dbyangs) rin chhen nas a rag dang lag sha byung, sme (smre) nas don sing lag sha chhe byung rten mani bdun (dun) brgya (rgya) dang nyer bdun yod. byang chhub (chhung) mchhod rten gching yod. bkra shis bsam byor dang. bstan dsin bu srid dang tshe bai mchhog rgyur !!

Translation

Who looks upon (the living beings) with merciful eyes, to Lord Avalokitesvara, I pay obeisance. Ac ma ho! In the southern direction of the valley of Mount Tise (Kailash)...on the earth created Jambudvipa in the south..Singhu.Sing ge during the period when his crown is held high. The great king Dharam Singh in the castle at Khangsar, 'in a well developed country, his crown is held high. Here at Bog (village) where ten virtues meet, from the lineage of Gyanshing (wood-ornament) whose origin is well established and renowned...the eldest Chhoskyid, mother Sonam, elder brother Ngos dub. younger brother Dondub, younger sister Zangmo, great pon (painter) Phagspa Chhospel, Chhosjor, Dorje Rikyab, Lagshes Tshe dya. ma Ganzom, eldest son Tashi Samjor, Tanzin Bukhrid (daughter?), dearest Tshewang Tanzin and Padma Bukhrid, very kind sister-in-law, who for favour of virtue and prosperity offered, food, tea, cakes fried in deep oil, *chhang* and wine. Chhewang Tshewang Rinchhen offered wine and one quarter part of meat Tshering (from the house) of Domba offered generously food and *chhang*, from sMe village offered *chhang* and quarter part of sheep meat were received. There are (were raised) 7207 *mani* and one *mchod rten*.

Annexure I

Gemur Historical

Documents

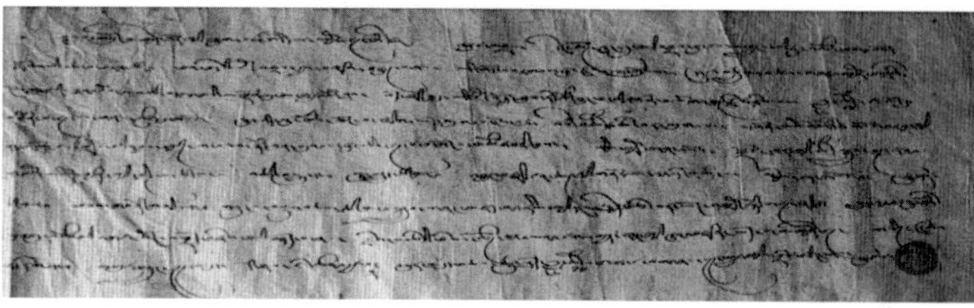

Transliteration

༄ བསླབ་གསུམ་མཁྱེན་ནོར་གྱི་ཕྱུག་པ་དཔལ་འཁོར་ལགས་རིན་པོ་ཆེ་གམ་དེར། འབུལ་འབྲས། དེང་ཚོགས་བྱང་དུ་མའི་འབྲས་དུ་ལས་འབྱུངས་པའི་སྐུ་འཚོ་དཔག་བསམ་ལྡོན་པའི་རྩ་བ་བརྟན་ཅིང་།ཕན་བདེའི་ལོ་འབྲས་རྒྱས་བཞིན་བཞུགས་པ་ནས། འདི་གདོང་བརྟག་པ་ཞུ་རྟེན་ལྷ་གསོ་དང་། དངུལ་བཅུ་དྲུག་བཅས་གནང་འཁོར་བཀྲིན་ཆེ། ངོས་བླ་མའི་ཐན་པོའང་འཆི་བདག་གི་བཀོན་དུ་མ་གྱུར་འཚམས་ནས། བོད་ཞིང་དུ་འདི་ལོ་སྐྱིད་ཐུབ་རེ་ཙམ་བྱུང་བ་ནི་དཀོན་མཆོག་ཐུགས་རྗེར་ཤེས་པས།ཟླ་༤ ཚེས་༡༧ ལ་ལམ་དུ་འཚོན་པ་ལགས་པས་གནས་ཚུལ་དུ་གསོལ། སྐུ་ཉིད་སྐུ་ཁམས་ཅོང་བ་ཞིག་ཡོད་འདུག་པ་ངོས་ཀྱང་། སེམས་འཚོ་ཏ་ཅང་ཆེ་བར་འདུག་པས། ལྷད་ཀོན་མཆོག་རིན་པོ་ཆེར་གསོལ་བཏབ་ཀྱི་ནད་གདོན་ལས་གྲོལ་བའི་སྐྱབས་དམིགས་གང་ཟབ་རྣམ་ཀུན་འདུན་པ་ཞུ་རྗེས་ལགས་པ་ལྷད་གོངས་མཆོར་བཟླ་བ་དང་། རིམ་གྲོ་གནང་འོས། སྒྲོལ་དཀར་གྱི་ཚེ་སྒྲུབ་རྟགས་ལྡན་ཞུ་འདོད་མཆོད་སྦྱིན་གྱི་དམིགས་པ་ཅི་མང་། འཆི་བསླུ་དང་། སྐུ་སྲུང་ཅི་མང་། འབྱུང་བཞི་ལན་ཆགས་ཀྱི་གཏོར་མ་ཀུང་(ཡང་)དེ་མཇུངས། སྐྱེས་ལྷ་གསོལ་བ། སྐུ་དོར་ཅི་མང་། ལྷབཀའ་ཐང་རྣམ་གཉིས་དང་། གཟུངས་བསྡུས་བཅས་ཅི་མང་སྒྲུབ་གནང་མཛད་ནས་རིམ་གྱིས་དངས་སྐྱེད་ཆེ་བར་ཡོང་འགྲོ་སྙམ་པ་ལགས་ཞིང་། སྐད་ཀྱང་ལྷ་སྐུ་རིན་པོ་ཆེ་ཡུན་དུ་འཚོ་བའི་འགལ་རྐྱེན་འཕྲོད་བཞེས་མི་སྟོད་པ་ནས། རྗེས་བརྩེའི་ཕེབས་ཚོགས་ཀྱང་ཡན་ལག་བརྒྱུད་ལྡན་གྱི་རྒྱུན་བཞིན་ཡོད་པ་མཁྱེན་ལགས། གཟིགས་རྟེན་ལྷ་རེག་དང་། མགུལ་བསྒྲུང་ཐུགས་མདུད། དམ་རྫས་ལེ་ཚན་རྒྱལ་བ་༢ ཕུར་མདུད་བཅས་ཆུ་སྟོད་ཟླ་༤ ཚེས་༡༧ ལ་ཏ་ལ་བག་ནས་ཐུགས་སྤྱལ་གྱིས་བྲིལ་བའི་དང་ནས་ཕུལ།

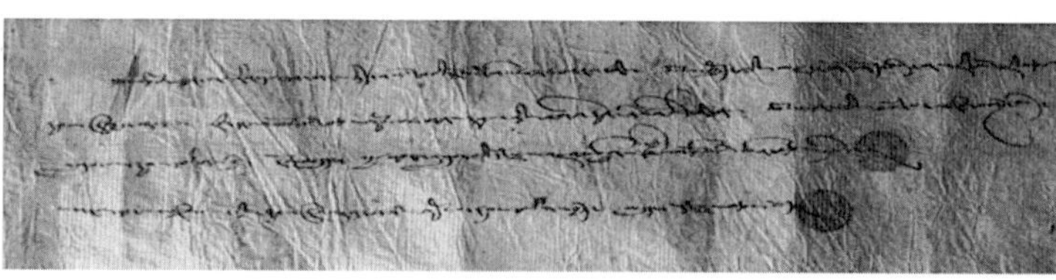

Transliteration

༄ དད་མཆོག་ལྡན་པ་བསྟན་འཛིན་དཔལ་ལྡན་གང་ཉིད་འཚོ་བའི་དངོས་པོ་གསེར་ལྟར་བཟང་ཞིང་། ཆོས་སྤྱོད་ཀྱིས་མཛད་སྒོ་སྟོད་མེད་ནས་རི་མོ་རྫི་སྤྱལ་སྐྱབས་རྟེན་དུ་ཕྱ་རྫས། རིན་དང་འཁོར་ལོ་བཅས་སྦྱོར་བར་གནས་སྐབས་ཀྱི་འགལ་རྐྱེན་ཞེར་འཚེ་ཞི་ནས། ཆོས་ལྡན་གྱི་བསམ་པ་བཞིན་བགེགས་མེད་འགྲུབ་པས་སྐྱབས་དམིགས་བྱེད། རྟེན་མདུད། ལྷ་རྒྱལ་དབང་འབྲུག་པའི་དམ་རྫས་འཛའ་ཚུགས་རིན་པོ་ཆེས་གཙོས་ལེ་ཚན་བཅས་སྤེལ། ཡང་ངག་དབང་འཕྲིན་ལས་ཀྱིས་སྐྱབས་རྟེན་འཛུག་གཉིས་སྦྱོར་པ་དམིགས་བྱེད། མདུད། དམ་རྫས་བཅས་ཡོད།

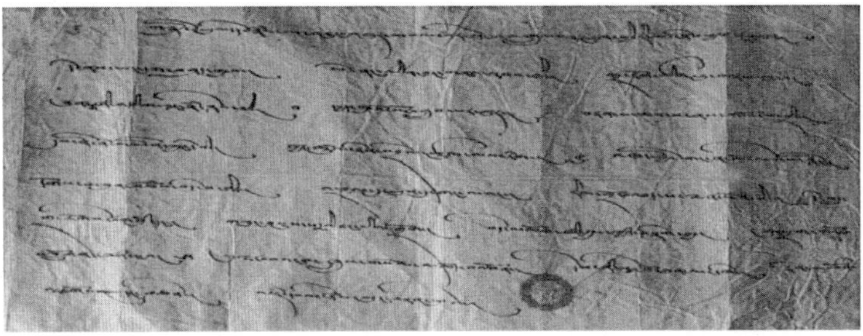

Transliteration

༄ ཀུན་ཁྱབ་ཀློང་ཡངས་ཆོས་ཀྱི་དབྱིངས་ཆེན་པོར། །ཡེ་ཤེས་རང་བྱུང་དག་པའི་ངོ་བོ་ཅན། །ཟབ་ཞི་སྤྲོས་བྲལ་ཉིད་ཀྱང་ཁྱབ་གདལ་མ། །ཡོངས་འགྲུབ་གདོད་མའི་མགོན་དེས་ཆེ་མཆོག་སྩོལ། །ངག་ལ་དབང་བ་འཇིགས་མེད་མཐུ་ཐོབ་པའི། །རྒྱལ་བསྟན་ཆོས་ཀྱི་ཉིན་བྱེད་དབང་པོ་དེ། །བཤད་སྒྲུབ་འཕྲིན་ལས་སྣང་བ་རྒྱས་པའི་ཕྱིར། །གཡོ་མེད་ངེས་པར་འཚོ་གཞེས་བརྟན་གྱུར་ཅིག །མཆོག་གསུམ་བདེན་པའི་བྱིན་རླབས་གྲུ་(འགྲུ་)ཆར་རྒྱུན། །བསྐལ་བཟང་གདུལ་བྱའི་ཡིད་མཆོར་བབས་པ་ལས། །མོས་དགེའི་སྨྱུ་གུ་ཕུན་ཚོགས་དར་དྲག་པའི། །གསོལ་བཏབ་རེ་འབྲས་ཏུག་བརྟན་རྒྱས་གྱུར་ཅིག །ཅེས་པའང་ཡོངས་འཛིན་ཞུ་པས་དང་སྦྱོངས་འབར་བཞིན་རྒྱུ་སྐོན་ཚོགས་འབུལ་བ་འདོད་པའི་དོན་ཀུན་ནས་འགྲུབ་པའི་དབྱིད་དམ་པར་གྱུར་ཅིག །ཀཱ་ལྱཱ་ཎ་ཝརྡྷནྟུ།

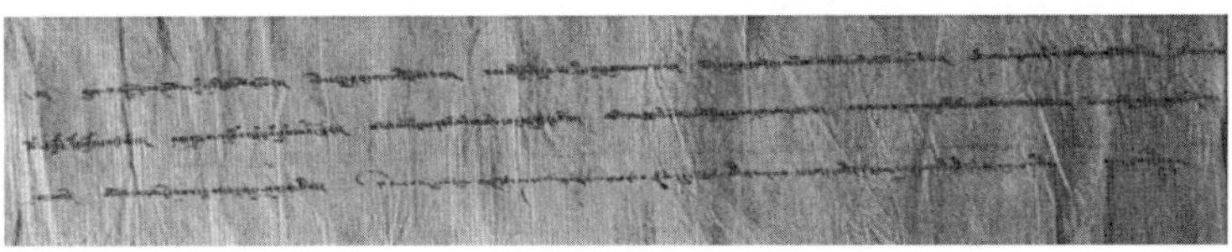

Transliteration

༄ གཉའི་ཡུལ་དཔོན་རྣམས་ལ་འབྱུང་འགྱུར་གསལ་བར་བྱེད་པ་འཕྲུལ་སྣང་རྒྱན་གྱི་རི་མོ་ཞེས་བྱ་བ་བཞུགས་སོ།།

དེ་ནས་ཡང་དག་བཤད་བྱ་བ། །ཡེ་སྣང་མིན་ཀྱང་གནས་སྐབས་ཀྱི། །སྒྲ་རྟོག་ཚིག་ཏུ་བརྗོ་བས་བྱུང་། །ཀུན་གཞི་གཅིག་ཀྱང་རྣམ་ཤེས་ཀྱི། །དབྱེད་བྱ་སོ་སོར་གྲུབ་པར་གྱུར། །བརྟན་པ་ཆགས་ནས་གཡོ་བ་སྲིད། །དུས་ནི་ཉོ་བ་མིན་ཀྱང་དེའི། །སྤྱོད་ཚུལ་རྟེན་འབྲེལ་ཚུལ་ལས་རེག །འབད་ཀྱི་གང་ན་ལམ་ལེགས་

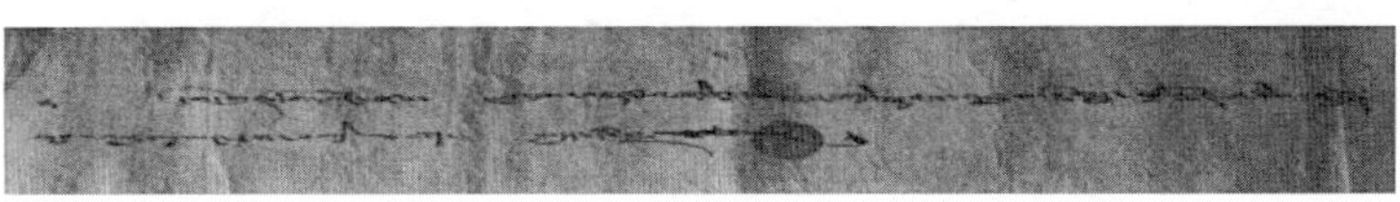

Transliteration

༄ དགེ་ཟུར་དགེ་སློང་ནས། བླ་མ་བསྟན་འཛིན་དཔལ་ལྡན་གྱི་སྐྱབས་འཇུག་རྗེན་དུ་ཕྱི་སྐོར་གཅིག་འཁོར་སྐྱབས་འཇུག་ཡང་དག་བགྱིས་ཡོད། མཎྜད་དམ་རྫས་བཅས།

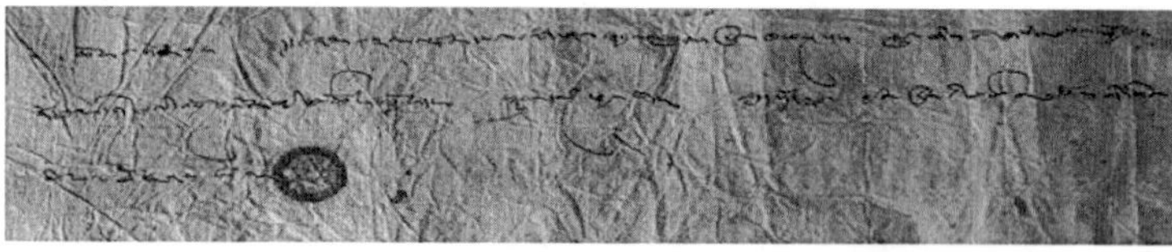

Transliteration

༄ ཆོས་འཛིན་པར། དད་ལྡན་བསྟན་འཛིན་དཔལ་ལྡན་ནས་སྐྱབས་འཇུག་རྟེན་ཁ་བཏགས་དང་། དངུལ་གིར་མོ་(སྒོར་མོ་)གཅིག་བཙོལ་(སྩལ་)འབྱོར་པར་རྣམ་ཀུན་དགེ་བའི་བསྔོ་རྟེན་གྱི་མཚམས་སྦྱོར་དང་། སྐྱབས་དམིགས་བྱས་ཡོད། མདུད་དམ་རྒྱས། བྱིན་རྟེན་ལེ་མཚན་བཅས་བདེ་ཆེན་ཆོས་འཁོར་ནས་སྤྲེལ།

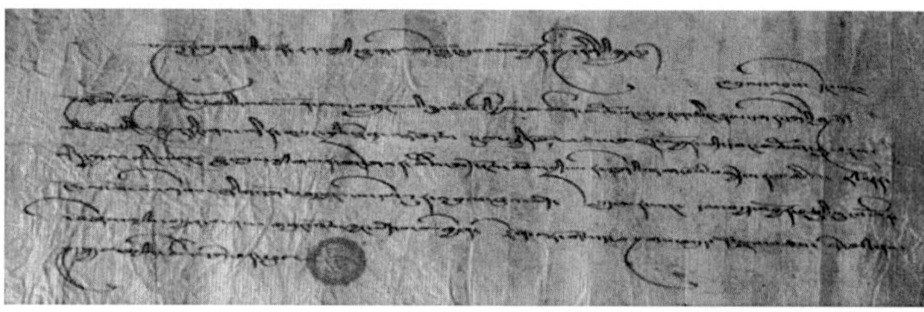

Transliteration

༄ འཕགས་ནོར་བདུན་གྱི་ཡོན་ཏན་གྱི་ཕྱུག་པ་དགེ་སློང་དཔལ་འབྱོར་ལགས་རིན་པོ་ཆེའི་སྐུ་དྲུང་དུ་འབུལ་འབྲས། དེང་ཡང་སྔོན་དགེ་ཚོགས་གཉིས་དུ་མའི་དཔལ་ཡོན་ལས་འཁྲུངས་པའི་སྐུ་འཚོའི་རྒྱལ་མཚན་མཆོག་ཏུ་བརྟན་ཅིང་རྣམ་དཀར་དགེ་བའི་ཐུགས་དམ་མི་ཉམས་ཅིང་བཞུགས་རིང་ནས་འདིར་གསུང་ཕྲིན་རྟེན་ལྷ་གོས། དངུལ་སྒོར་མོ་གཅིག་བཅས་མཇལ་འབྱོར་ཡིད་དབང་མཆོག་ཏུ་བརྟས། འདིར་སྐྱུལ་མིང་པའང་། སྐུ་ལུས་ཀྱི་གཡར་ཁང་གསར་ཆོས་མཛོད་ངོས་ཆོས་སྲིད་ཡར་དགེའི་ལྷག་བསམ་བསྐྱེད་པར་མཆིས། ཟེ་ལྟར་ཟབ་བཞེས་ཀྱིས་བརྒྱུད་པ་ནས་གསུང་འོས་ཀྱང་ཡོད་པ་མཆིས། རྟེན་ལྷ་གོས་དང་། ཐུགས་མདུད། དམ་རྒྱས་བཅས། ཏེ་མི་ནས་ཐུགས་སྐྱུལ་གྱིས་ཆོས་དགེ་བར་ཕུལ།

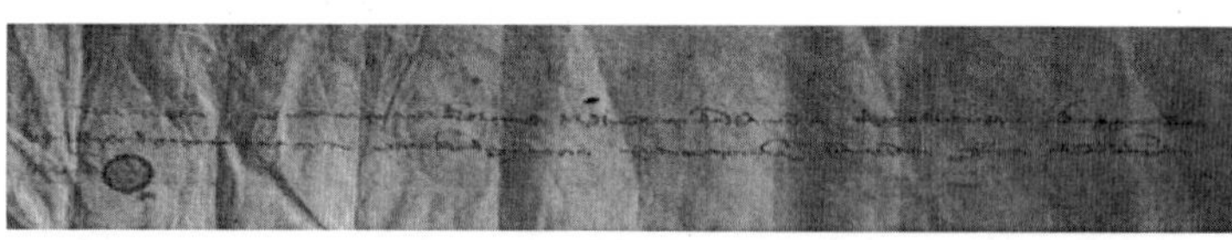

Transliteration

༄ བདེ་ཆོས་ཡོངས་འཛིན་པར། དད་སྟོབས་ལྡན་པ་དཀར་ཞུ་དཔལ་འབྱོར་ཚོ་ཁམས་བཟང་ཞིང་། ཆོས་སྤྱོད་འཕེལ་བ་ནས་ཡི་གེ་རྟེན་ལྷ་རེག་དང་། གིར་(སྒོར་)དངུལ་གཉིས་བཅས་འབྱོར་པར། འདི་ནས་བྱང་ཆུབ་མ་ཐོབ་བར་དུ་དགེ་ཞིང་ཤེས་པའི་སྐྱབས་འཇུག་གནད་སྨིན་བྱས་ཡོད། སླད་མར་འཚོ་བའི་མཐུན་འཇུག་དང་། འཕྲོས་འོས་ཀྱང་ཡོད་པ་འཚལ། རྟེན་ལྷ་རེག་དང་། བསྲུང་མདུད། བྱིན་རྟེན་ལེ་མཚན་བཅས་སྤྲེལ་བ་དགེ།

Transliteration

༄ བསླབ་གསུམ་ཧུར་སྒྲིག་འཛིན་པ་དགེ་སློང་དཔལ་འབྱོར་ལགས་རིན་པོ་ཆེའི་དྲུང་དུ། སྙན་འབུལ། དེང་ཡང་།

ཚོགས་གཉིས་རྒྱ་མཚོའི་དཔལ་ཡོན་ལས་འོངས་པའི་སྐུ་འཚོ་སྐྱོང་པོའི་ཟླ་བ་རབ་དུ་(ཏུ་)་བརྟན་ཅིང་རྣམ་དགེའི་ཐུགས་དམ་མི་ཀློད་ཅིང་བཞུགས་པ་ནས་ འདིར་ཕྱག་ཕྲིན་རྟེན་ལྷ་རེག་དང་། དངུལ་ཕྱིར་མོ་གཅིག་བཅས་འབྱོར་པ་ཡིད་བསོས་སུ་གྱུར། འདིར་ནའང་བདེ་ཐུས་ནས་བསྟན་འགྲོའི་ལྷག་བསམ་མི་ དམན་པར་མཆིས། མཚམས་དོན། ཇི་ལྟར་བླ་ལོ་གསོལ་འདེབས་དཔེ་ཆ་དགོས་གསུང་པ་སྔོན་དུ་དེ་ཁའི་མི་སྣ་ཕྱིར་ལོག་གཏོང་འབུལ་ལམ་ཞུས་ཚར་བའི་ དགོངས་བཞུགས་དང་། གར་ཤའི་གནས་ཡིག་དཔེ་ཆ་དང་མ་ཟད་ཐུགས་ལོའི་དཔེ་ཆ་རེ་དགོས་རྩལ་ཕེབས་པ། ད་ཆ་ལག་ཐོག་ཏུ་དཔེ་ཆ་ཕྱོལ་ཟེབ་སོགས་ མི་འདུག་ཅིང་རྗེས་སུ་བྱུང་ཚེ་འབུལ་ལམ་ཞུས་ཆོག་པ་དང་། སྙད་མར་ཡང་། དལ་བརྒྱད་འབྱོར་བཅུའི་སྐུ་འཚོར་མཐུན་འཛུག་དང་། ནང་མའི་བཀའ་ལུང་ འོས་ཀུང་ཞལ་འགྲོའི་དཔལ་རྒྱུན་བཞིན་ཡོད་པ་མཁྱེན་འཚལ། རྟེན་ལྷ་གོས་དང་ཐུགས་མདུད་བཅས། ཐུགས་སྨོལ་གྱིས་ཚེས་བཟང་པོར་ཕུལ་བ་དགེ།

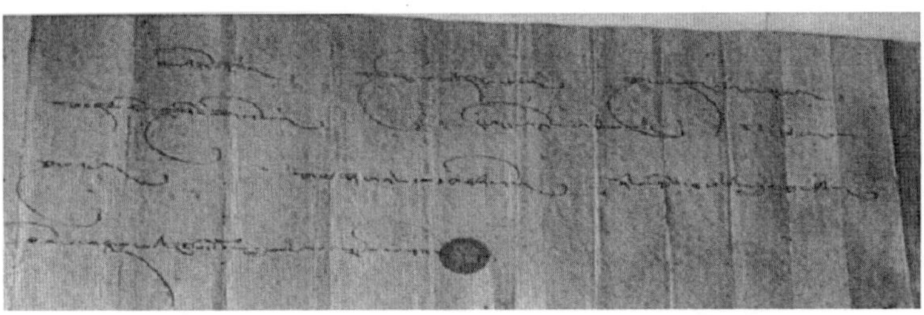

Transliteration

༄ དག་པའི་རྡོ་རྗེ་བཅོམ་ལྡན་འདས། །སྣ་ཚོགས་གཟུགས་ཀྱི་རོལ་པ་ཅན། །ཕྱོགས་ཀུན་འགྲོ་བ་དུལ་(འདུལ་ཡངས་)སྣང་བ། །ཡོངས་འཛིན་ཞེས་གྲགས་ དེར་གསོལ་འདེབས། །རང་བྱུང་ཤེས་པའི་རིག་པ་ཡི། །ཆོས་ཀུན་མ་ལུས་རྟོགས་པ་དང་། །བདག་གཞན་དོན་གཉིས་མཐར་ཕྱིན་ཏེ། །རྣམ་མཁྱེན་སྐུ་བཞི་ འགྲུབ་གྱུར་ཅིག །ཅེས་པ་གཎྜ་གྲ་པའི་ངོར་བདེ་ཆོས་བླ་མིང་པས་བྲིས་པ་དགེ།

Transliteration

༄ ཚོག་སྤྲུལ་པར། དད་མོས་ལྡན་པ་འཕྲིན་ལས་ནས་སྐྱབས་རྟེན་ཨ་ན་གཅིག་འབྱོར། མི་འདོད་ཉེ་ཚེ་ཞི་ནས་ཚེ་དབང་ཡོངས་རྫོགས་རྒྱས་པའི་དམིགས་འདུན་ ཕྱེད། མདུད་དམ་བཅས་རི་ཁྲོད་ནས་དགེ།

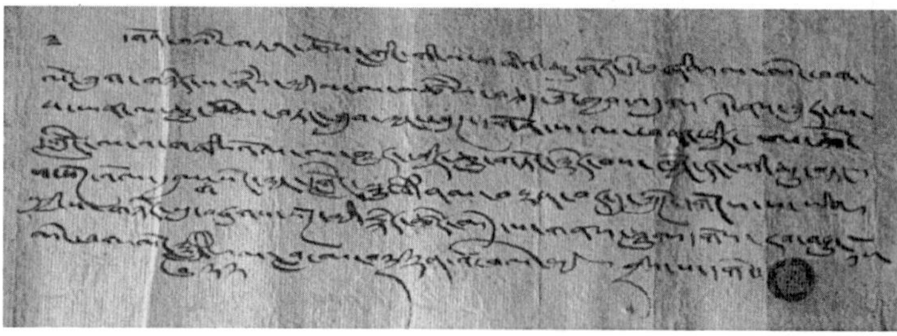

Transliteration

༈ དགོན་བསམ་གཏན་ཆོས་གླིང་གི་ས་གཞིའི་ཆུ་ནོར་དེ་བཞིན་ལ་མོ་ཁག་པོ་ཐུག་གཉེར་པ་རྣམས་ཀྱི་ས་ལ་མཚམས་བཅད་ཐོ་རྒྱབ་འདུག །དེ་ནས་ཐུར་མ་ས་ཡན་ལ་ཆུ་ཙམ་བཏང་ཐུབ་ཀྱང་། ཐུགས་དགོན་པ་ལ་ཕན་ཕྱིར། ཨ་ཙོ་དགེ་སློང་ལ་ས་གཞི་དགོན་ལ་ཕྱུར་ཕྱིར་ཆུ་གཏོང་ཐེར་བས་ཁྱོང་(ཁྱོད་)རང་གི་ཆུ་བཏངས་ས་སོགས་འོལ་རྒྱལ་བ་སོང་ཀྱང་དགེ་སློང་སྐུ་ཚེ་ནམ་བརྟན་བར་དུ་ཐུགས་རྗེ་དགོངས་པ་ཡིན། ཕྱི་ས་གཉེར་སུ་བཞུགས་སོགས་ཀྱི་སྐོར་ཚོར་མེད་པ་གནས་ཐུག(བཅུག་)དགོས། རབ་འབྱུང་༡༥ མེ་ཕག་ལོ་ཟླ་༨ ཚེས་༢༢ ལ་བླ་མ་བཀྲིས་བརྟན་འཕེལ་གྱིས་ཕྲིས་པ་དགེ།

Transliteration

༈ དགེ་བའི་བློ་གྲོས་ཀྱི་འཇུག་པ་མི་དམན་པ་གར་ཞ་དགོན་འབངས་ཚང་མ་འཚོ་བ་བླ་བའི་དཔལ་ལྟར་ཀུན་ཏུ་གཙང་ཞིང་། རྣམ་དཀར་དོན་ཡོད་ཀྱི་བགྱི་བ་མི་དམན་པ་ནས། རི་མོ་རྟེན། ཇོ་བོའི་སྐུ་དང་། དངུལ་གསུམ། འཛོན་ལྟར་བཅས་འགྱུར་པ་ཡིད་སྨྲོ། འདིར་ཡང་འདུ་ཁམས་བདེ་ཞིང་དགེ་སྦྱོར་ལ་བརྩོན་པར་འཚལ། ཚེད་དོན། ཉེ་ལམ་ཡི་གེ་འབྱོར་དོན། གཉའ་འཕགས་པ་རིན་པོ་ཆེའི་བཞུགས་ཁང་དབུ་ཐོག་ཏུ་གཟི་ར་ཞིག་གསར་གཟོ་(བཟོ་)བགྱི་དགོས་ཅེས་པ་དེ་བཞིན། གཞི་བབ་སྐུ་རྟེན་ནད་པར་ཙན་དེ་རིགས་ལ་འབུལ་རྒྱུ་བྱུང་ན། རང་ཉིད་ཚོགས་རྫོགས་པར་བྱེད་པའི་རང་བཞིན་དུ་འབུམས་ནའང་། ས་ཁང་འགྲུང་ཞིང་། འགྲོགས་འགྲོགས་སུ་མ་གྲུབ་པ། དེ་བས་ན་སྐད་ན་གཟི་ར་དེ་ལྟ་ཞིག་སྒྲུབ་འདུན་སེམས་ལ་བཞག་བྱེད་པ་དང་། འཕྲལ་དུ་

ནི་མ་ཐུབ་པ་བྲེལ་བ་མེད་པ་འཚལ། སྐད་ཀྱང་འཚོ་བར་ཟབ་ཅིང་། རྣམ་དཀར་གྱི་བགྱི་བ་ཡར་ཟླན་དུ་འཚལ་ཞིང་འཕྲོས་འོས་ཀྱང་བགྱི། རྟེན་ཁ་བཏགས། བསྐྱུང་མདུད་བཅས། དབེན་གར་ཞ་ནས་ཆོས་ལ་དགེ།

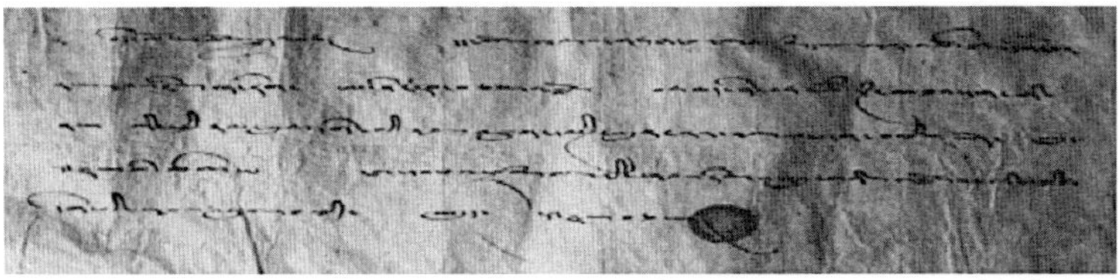

Transliteration

༄ བདེ་ཆོས་ཆོས་སྐྱིལ་བར། དང་མོས་ལྡན་པ་གར་ཞ་བསྟན་འཛིན་དཔལ་ལྡན་འཚོ་ཁམས་དགེ་བ་ནས་སྐྱབས་རྟེན་ལྷ་རེག །ཨ་ཤེ་རབ་བཅས་འབྱོར། བར་ཆད་ཉེ་བར་འཚེ་རིགས་མཐའ་དག་ཞི་ནས། འདི་ཕྱི་རྣམ་ཀུན་དགེ་བའི་སྐྱབས་འཛུག་དམིགས་འདུན་ནན་ཏན་ཡང་དག་བགྱིས་ཡོད། མདུད་དམ་རྫས་ལེ་ཚན་དང་། ངག་དབང་འཕྲིན་ལས་ཀྱི་སྐྱབས་རྟེན་འཛུ་གཉིས་འབྱོར་པ་འདི་ཕྱིར་དགེ་བའི་སྐྱབས་འཛུག་བགྱིད། མདུད། དམ་རྫས་བཅས།

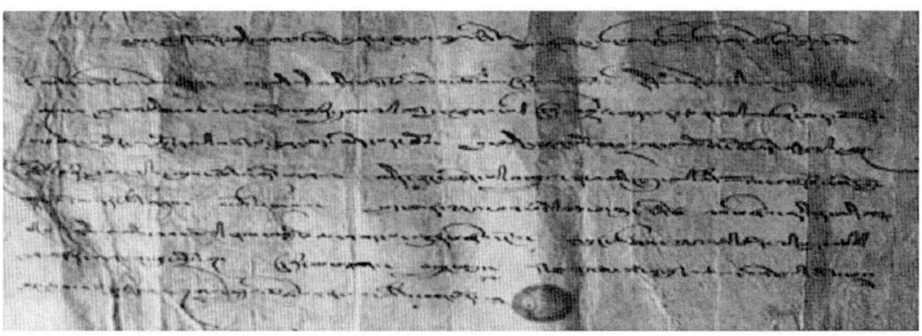

Transliteration

༄ བསླབ་གསུམ་ཡོན་ཏན་གྱི་ཕྱུག་པ་དགེ་འདུན་བཙུན་པ་ལྡན་རྒྱས་རིན་པོ་ཆེའི་གམ་དེར།འབྲུལ་འབྲས་དེང་ཚང་མ་སྐུ་འཚོ་དགེ་ཞིང་ཆོས་སྐྱོང་དགེ་ལེགས་གོང་འཕེལ་ནས། བང་མི་འདི་གཉིས་གདོངས་ཕེབས་ཚོགས་རྟེན་ལྷ་གོས། རིན་ཆེན་གཉིས་པ་དངུལ་སྒྲིར་མོ་ཤྲ་དང་། དངུལ་གཅིག་བཅས་པ་རོལ་ཕྱིན་དྲུགས་ཀྱི་(དྲུག་གི་)ལམ་དུ་བཞུགས་པའི་རྟེན་འབྲེལ་ཁྱད་པར་ཅན་གྱི་མཚན་མར་མངོན་པ་བཅས་འབྱོར་པ་སྤྲོ་བའི་བསམ་པ་རྒྱུན་ཆད་མེད་པར་ཐོབ། ལྷ་མིང་རྒན་པོ་ཀུང་(ཡང་) ལྡན་མཆོག་རྡོ་རྗེ་འཆང་དེ་ཉིད་ཀྱི་ཐུགས་རྗེའི་བྱིན་རླབས་ཀྱིས་ལུས་ཁམས་བདེ་བ་ནས། འདིར་སྣང་ཞེན་པའི་འཁྲུལ་སྣང་གི་

ངང་དུ་མི་ཚེ་ཡོལ་བཞིན་དགེ་སློ་ཕྲ་མོ་མ་དོར་ཙམ་གནས། མཚམས་འབྲས། སྣད་མར་ཀུང་(ཡང་)ཕན་བདེའི་རྩ་བ་སྐུ་རིན་པོ་ཆེར། ཟབ་བཞེས་ཐེ་དོར་མོ་སྐྱོད་ཅིང་། རིམ་གཉིས་ཟབ་མོའི་རྣལ་འབྱོར་ལ་འབད་པ་ཕྱུར་བཞེས་དོས། གསུང་ཚོགས་ཀུང་འཆི་མེད་ཀྱི་བདུད་རྩིའི་རྒྱུན་བཞིན་གནང་བ་ཞུ་སྨྲོ་ལགས། རྟེན་ཁ་བཏགས། བསྔུང་མདུད་༡༧ དམ་རྫས་ཤོག་སྨམ་གསུམ་བཅས་ལྡེ་མི་ཆོས་གྲྭ་བྱང་ཆུབ་བསམ་གླིང་ནས་ཐུགས་སྐྱུལ་རྡོ་རྗེ་འཛིན་པས་ཆོས་བཟང་པོར་ཕུལ།

Transliteration

༄ གཏན་འགྲོའི་དཔལ་མགོན་ལ་སྐྱབས་མགོན་ལ་རྒྱལ་བའི་དབང་པོ་འབྲུག་པ་རིན་པོ་ཆེ་མཆོག་གི་ཞབས་པད་མངོན་པར་ཛོ་(མཛོ་)བའི་ཁྲི་དྲུང་དུ། འདིར་གསལ་གྱི་དངོས་པོ་འབྱོར་པར། གནས་སྐབས་ཉེར་འཚོ་ཞི་ཞིང་། མཐུན་རྐྱེན་ལེགས་ཚོགས་འཕེལ་བའི་སྐྱབས་དམིགས་གང་ལག་བགྱིས་ཡོད། མདུད་དང་། ཕྱིན་ཐུན་ལེ་ཚན་༢ བཅས་སྤེལ་མཆོག་གསུམ་གུས་པ་གསེར་བཞུགས་བྱུང་བ་དཔལ་འབྱོར་གྱི་ལྷ་ཕྱག་གྲངས་དང་བཅས་དེ་ལ་སྐྱབས་འཛུག་དོ་རྗེའི་གུར་ཁྲིམ་ནས་མི་འདོར་བ་མཁྱེན། ཞུ་རྒྱུར་རིན་གཉིས་སྤྲིར་མོ་གཉིས་འབུལ་ལམ་ཞུས་ལགས་ན། མི་དོག་ལྷ་རྫས་སུ་སྨིན་པ་ནས་རྟགས་རྫེས་སྐྱབ་ལམ་དུ་འཛུག་པས་བཀའ་བཟང་འབྱམས་ལ་(ལས་)ཀྱང་རྩོལ་བ་མཁྱེན། མཁྱེན། བཞེས་(ཞེས་)གསོལ་བ་འདེབས་བརྟེན་ལྷ་ཡི་རིག་བྱ་བཅས་ཕུལ་བའི་ཞུ།

Transliteration

༄ བསྟན་པའི་བདག་པོ་ལ་སྐྱབས་མགོན་འབྲུག་པ་རིན་པོ་ཆེའི་གསེར་ཁྲིའི་དྲུང་དེ།

Transliteration

༄ བསྟན་པའི་བདག་པོ་སྐྱབས་མགོན་འབྲུག་པ་རིན་པོ་ཆེའི་གསེར་ཁྲིའི་དྲུང་དེ། ༄ གདན་འགྲོའི་དཔལ་མགོན་སྐྱབས་མགོན་རྒྱལ་བའི་དབང་པོ་
འབྲུག་པ་རིན་པོ་ཆེ་མཆོག་གི་ཞབས་པད་མཚན་པར་ཐོ་(མཐོ་)བའི་ཁྲི་དྲུང་དུ། འདིར་གསལ་གྱི་དངོས་པོ་འབྱོར་པར། གནས་སྐབས་ཉེར་འཚོ་ཞི་
ཞིང་།མཐུན་རྐྱེན་ལེགས་ཚོགས་འཕེལ་བའི་བས་དམིགས་གང་ཡག་བགྱིས་ཡོད། མདུད་དང་། ཕྱིན་ཕྲན་ལེ་ཚན་༢ བཅས་སྤེལ་མཆོག་གསུམ་གུས་པ་གསེར་
བསྒུགས་ཕྱུང་བ་དཔལ་འབྱོར་གྱི་ལྷ་ཕྱག་གྲངས་དང་བཅས་དེ་སྐྱབས་འཇུག་རྡོ་རྗེའི་གུར་ཁྱིམ་ནས་མི་འདོར་བ་མཁྱེན། ཞུ་རྒྱུར་རིན་གཉིས་སྙིང་མོ་གཉིས་
འབུལ་ལམ་ཞུས་ལགས་ན། མི་དོག་ལྷ་རྫས་སུ་སྨིན་པ་ནས་ཐུགས་རྗེས་སྐྱོན་ལམ་དུ་འཇུག་པས་བཀའ་བཟང་འབྱམས་ལ་(ལས་)ཀྱང་རྫོལ་བ་མཁྱེན། མཁྱེན།
བཞེས་(ཞེས་)གསོལ་བ་འདེབས་བརྟེན་ལྷ་ཡི་རིག་བྱ་བཅས་ཕུལ་བའི་ཞུ།

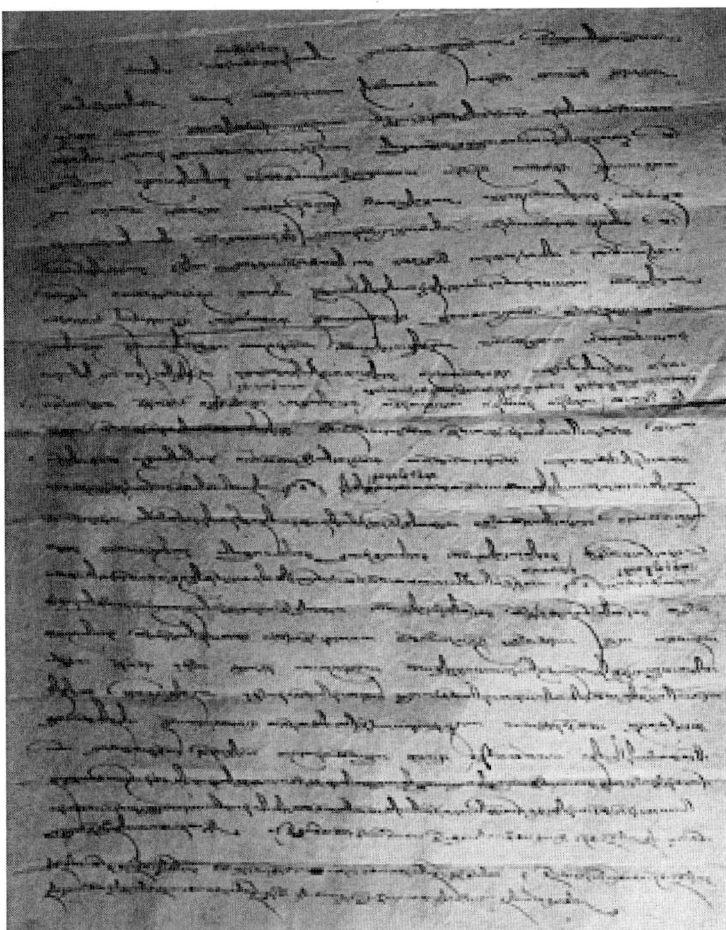

Transliteration

༡ ཨོཾ་སྭ་སྟི། {ཡོངས་འཛིན་རིན་པོ་ཆེ་ནས།} ཡབ་རེ་མཐོང་(ཐོང་) ཀུང་ཤྲིད་པ་ཡི། རྒྱ་མཚོ་ཆེ་ལས་སྤྲུལ་བྱེད་པས། ཡེ་ཤེས་གྲུབ་པའི་ཞལ་སྔ་ནས། ཐོབ་པའི་
བརྗེད་བྱང་འདི་ནའོ། ཐོག་མར། མཆོད་བརྗོད་རབ་བསལ། རིགས་རྣམས་མ་བཅས། བཟང་སྤྱོད། བྱམས་སྨོན། སྤྱོད་འཇུག །བདེ་བ་ཅན། མངོན་དགའ། སྨོན་
ལམ་རིང་མོ་ཆེ་རབ་མ་དང་འབྲེལ་མ། མི་སྐྱོད་པ་ཟུར་བཀོད་ཀྱི་མཆོད་བསྟོད། བར་དོའི་གསོལ་འདེབས་བཅས། ཚར་གཉིས། དྲག་དམར། བླ་མ་མཆོད་པ་
ལྷན་ཐབས་དང་འབྲེལ་མ། ཡིག་དྲུག་བསྒོམ་བཟླས་སྒྲུབ་ཐབས་གསེར་གྱི་འཕྲང་(འཕྲེང་) བ་ཚར་གཉིས། ཆོ་ག་རྡོ་རྗེ་རྒྱ་མདུད། མཆོད་པ་བཞི་མའི་ལུང་གཉིས།
གོང་ནོན་ཞེས་པ་ལྷན་སྐྱེས་སྒྲུབ་ཐབས། མངོན་རྟོགས། མཆོད་བསྟོད། ཕྱོགས་ལས་རྣམས་(རྣམ་) རྒྱལ། དབང་མཆོག །ལྷ་མོས་ལུང་། བསྟན་དགྲ་འཇོམས་བྱེད།

དམ་ཅན་སྤྱི་བསྐུལ། བསྐང་བཤགས་འོག་མིན་ལུང་། མཆོག་ཕྲན་ཟུར་བཀོད་གདོང་བཞི། མ་ནིང་། གཏོར་འབུལ་གསར་སྙིང་(སྙིང་)། འགྲུབ་པར་མོ་རྒྱས་
ཐུས་(བཐུས་)གཉིས། འཇམ་དཔལ་ཆོ་བདག །ཕྱུགས་ཐེག །ཚེ་དཔག་མེད་ཞི་བ་ལྷ་མང་། བཅུ་གཉིས་མ། དྲུག་ཅུ་མ་དངོས་གཞི། དབང་། སྨན་བརྒྱུད་རྡོ་
རྗེ། དཔལ་ལྡན་ཚོགས་གཉིས། དགེ་བས་ལེགས་བྱས། ལྷན་སྐྱེས། པག་མོ་ལྷ་མོ་བཅོ་ལྔ། སྔག་(བཏག)གཉིས། སྔོན་འགྲོའི་ཟིན་བྲིས་ཚར་གཉིས་ཁྲིད་དང་
བཅས་དགྱེས་པར་བཅས་ནས། དགོན་མཆོག་སྤྱི་འདུས། བགོར་(དགོར་)བཤགས། དྲི་མེད་བཤགས་རྒྱུད། གུ་རུ་མཚན་བརྒྱད། སྒྲོལ་མ་མཚན་བརྒྱད།
སྐྱབས་ཐབས་རྒྱ་མཚོ། རྣམས་འཇོམས་འབྲུས་མདོ། བརྒྱ་ཞི་མདོ་ལུགས། སྒྲོལ་མ་བཀྲིས་དོན་གྲུབ། བག་ཆགས་རང་གྲོལ། དགོན་མཆོག་སྤྱི་འདུས་སྦྱིན་སྲེག །
ལྷ་མོ་ནོར་རྒྱུན་མ། ཀུན་མཁྱེན་པད་དཀར་མཛད་པའི་ཞི་རྒྱས་དབང་དྲག་གི་སྦྱིན་སྲེག {བླ་མེད་ལུགས་ཀྱི་རབ་གནས།} མཐུན་མོང་བཞི་ཡི་རབ་གནས་ཀྱི་
ལུང་། {ཀརྨ་པའི་བཀའ་འབུམ་ཆ་ཚང་དུས་གསུམ་མཁྱེན་པའི་མཛད་པ། པོ་(འཕོ་)བའི་ལུང་། ཐོས་གྲོལ། སྨན་དཔེ་རྩ་བརྒྱུད། སྤྱན་རས་གཟིགས་ཀྱི་རྗེས་
གནང་།} བསྔོ་བས་ཡོན་བཤད། བསང་དཔེ་བཀྲིས་རེ་སྐོང་། གསོལ་འདེབས་ལེ་བདུན། ཛོར་གཏོད། ཟ་བྱེད་རྡོ་རྗེ་མགྲོ(གྲོ་)། གུ་རུ་ཚིག་བདུན། གཏེར་མ་
བརྒྱ་རྩ། འཛམ་གསེར། འཛམ་ནག །ཆ་གསུམ། རྡོ་རྗེ་གོ་ཁྲབ། རྗེས་གནང་ཞེར་གཉིས་མ་བཅས་ཀྱི་ལུང་དང་། རྣམས་(རྣམ་)འཇོམས་དབང་ཆེན། རྗེས་
གནང་ཞེར་གཉིས་མའི་དབང་ཆེན། ཚེ་དཔག་མེད་ཀྱི་དབང་ཆེན། མཆོད་པ་བཞི་མའི་དབང་། བདེ་མཆོག་བཅུ་གསུམ་མའི་དབང་ཆེན། མགོན་པོས་དབང་
ཆེན། དཔལ་ལྡན་ལྷ་མོ་ཡི་རྗེས་གནང་བཅས་གོང་ལྟར་ནོར་བ་མེད་པར་ཐོབ་པའི་ཐོ་ཡིག་བཀྲིས།

༢ {རྒྱལ་ཐྲས་རིན་པོ་ཆེ་ནས།} རིགས་ཀྱི་ཁྱབ་བདག་མཚན་མཐོང་(ཐོས་)པ་ཙམ་གྱི་སྒྲིབ་པ་ཡོངས་སུ་དག་ཅིང་འབྲས་བུ་མངོན་དུ་གྱུར་པ། མི་ཕམ་ཆོས་
དབང་རིག་འཛིན་འཕྲིན་ལས་བསྟན་འཛིན་མི་འགྱུར་རྡོ་རྗེ་ཀྱི་(འི་)གནང་བ། བླ་མ་མཆོད་པའི་དབང་ལུང་། བདེ་མཆོག་ལྷ་རྒྱས་དབང་ལུང་། ལྷ་མོ་བཅོ་
ལྔའི་དབང་། མི་འཁྲུགས་པའི་དབང་། དྲུག་ཅུ་མའི་དབང་། དགོན་མཆོག་སྤྱི་འདུས་ཀྱི་དབང་། {མདོ་མང་ཆ་ཚང་ལུང་།} གཏུམ་མོས་མེ་དབང་། མགོན་
པོའི་དབང་ཆེན་བཅས་ཐུགས་ཀྱི་ཞེས་སུ་འཛིན་ཅིང་དགྱེས་པ་ཆེན་པོས་གསལ་བ་ཡིན་པའི་བརྗེད་བྱང་།

༣ {ཐུགས་སྲས་རིན་པོ་ཆེ་ནས།} སློབ་དཔོན་ཆེན་པོ་ཧཱུྃ་ཀཱ་ར་ཡི་རྣམས་(རྣམ་)པར་རོལ་བ་ཐུགས་སྲས་མི་པམ་ཐུ་ཐུ་སྟོབས་རྡོ་རྗེ་ཀྱི་(འི་)གནང་བ། དགོན་
མཆོག་སྤྱི་འདུས་ཀྱི་ཚེ་དབང་། ཚེ་ཧྲ་བཟུང་འབྲེལ་གྱི་ཚེ་དབང་། གཏུམ་པོ་ཁྲུང་ཁྲ་ཡི་དབང་། སེང་གདོང་མའི་རྗེས་གནང་། མཆོད་བརྗོད་རབ་གསལ།
སྨོན་ལམ་ཡོངས་རྫོགས། བླ་མ་མཆོད་པ། ལྷན་རྒྱས། མཐོང་(ཐོང་)གྲོལ། མི་སྐྱོད་པ། ཛོར་གཏོད། བཅུ་གསུམ་མ། ཚུ་གཏོར། བག་ཆགས་རང་གྲོལ། ཆོས་ཀྱི་
སྣང་བས་མཛད་པའི་སྔོན་འགྲོ་བཞི་སྦྱོར་རྒྱས་བསྡུས་གཉིས་ཀྱི་ཁྲིད་ལུང་། ལྷན་སྐྱེས་སྦྱིན་སྲེག(བསྲེག) །བཅུ་གསུམ་མར་བརྟེན་པའི་རབ་གནས། ལྷན་རྒྱས་
ལ་རྟེན་པའི་རབ་གནས་འདི་གཉིས་ཆོས་ཀྱི་སྣང་བའི་མཛད་པ་ཕྱག་ཆེན་ཟིན་བྲིས། སྒྲོལ་མ་མཚན་བརྒྱད། གཞེར་(ཞེར་) གཅིག་མའི་བསྐྱོད་པ་ཕན་ཡོན་
སྒྲགས་མ། བཀའ་འགྱུར་རོ་ཅོག །ཕྱོགས་བཅུའི་མུན་སེལ། རྒྱ་ནག་ལྷག་བཟློག །ཤེས་རབ་སྙིང་པོ། གདུགས་དཀར་མཆོག་སྒྲུབ། སྣང་བརྒྱུད། བཀྲིས་བརྩེགས་
པ། བཀྲིས་ཀྱི་རིམས་པ་ཕན་བདེའི་སྒྲ་དབྱངས་བཅས་ལེགས་པར་ཐོབ་ཅིང་ངོས་རང་གིས་ཀྱང་ཞུས་པ་ཐམས་ཅད་ཀྱང་རང་གིས་གང་ནུས་ཀྱི་སྒྲུབ་པ་བྱས་
ཤིང་བླ་མ་རྣམས་ལ་ཡང་དང་གསུམ་འགྱུར་བ་མེད་པར་གསོལ་འདེབས་རྒྱུན་དུ་འབད་པ་ཡིན་པར་འདི་ཉིད་ཀུན་ཐོས་པའི་ཚིག་ཅིང་ཡི་གེར་བཏབ་པའི་སྨོ་
མེད་ཀྱང་ཕྱི་རབས་དོན་གཉེར་དགའ་ཡི་སླད་དུ་བརྗེད་བྱང་དུ་བྲིས་པ་སརྦ་ཛ་ག་ཏམ།

[1] རྗེ་གྲུབ་ཆེན་བསོད་རྣམས་(ནམས་)ཡེ་ཤེས་ནས། རྗེ་ཙུན་མི་ལས་(ལའི་)རྣམ་ཐར་ཀུར་འབུམ། སྔོན་འགྲོའི་ལུང་ཁྲིད། ཕྱག་ཆེན་ཟིན་བྲིས། ཚེ་ཧྲ་བཟུང་འབྲེལ་
གྱི་ཚེ་དབང་། འཕོ་ལུང་དཀར་ཁྲུང་མདའ་འཕངས། བཅས་གནང་བའི་བརྗེད་བྱང་ཐོ་ཡིན།

[2] རྗེ་ངག་དབང་དགེ་འདུན་ནས་སྔོན་འགྲོའི་ལུང་ཁྲིད་རྒྱས་པ་ཆོས་ཀྱི་སྣང་བའི་མཛད་པ་བཅས་གནང་བའི་བརྗེད་བྱང་ཐོ། ཕྱིས་གསང་ཕུ་ཕུ་སློབ་རྣམས་
ལ་ཕན་ཕྱིར་བཀོད་པ། བཀྲིས་པར་གྱུར་ཅིག །

Annexure II

Gemur Gonpa Chham-yig

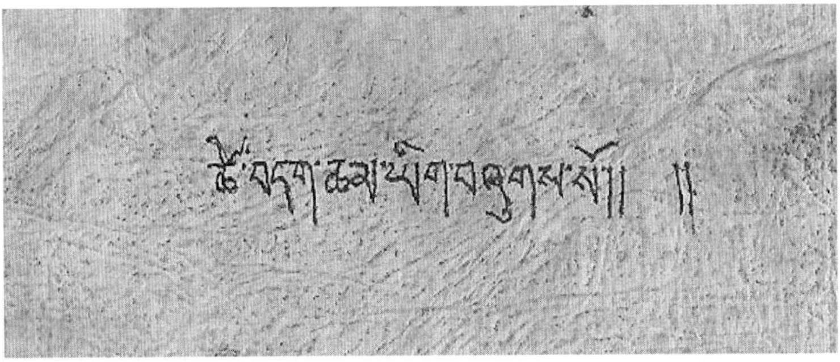

ཆོས་བདག་ཆམ་ཡིག་བཞུགས་སོ།། །།

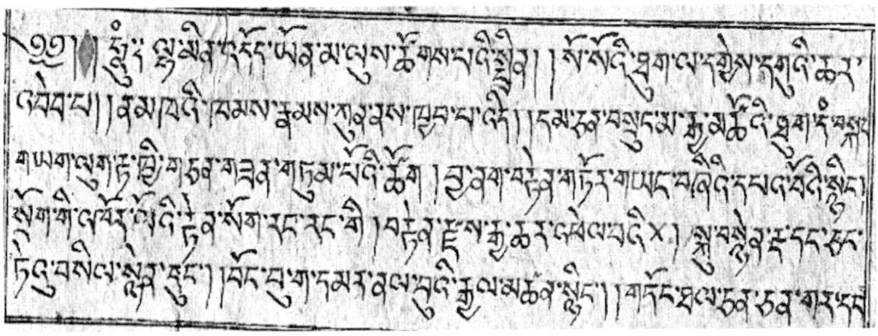

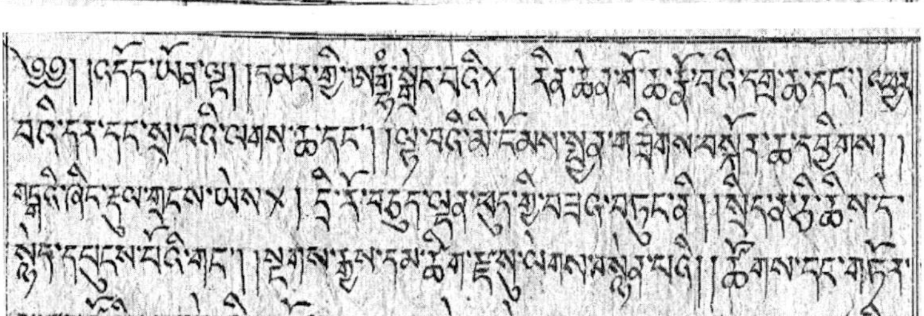

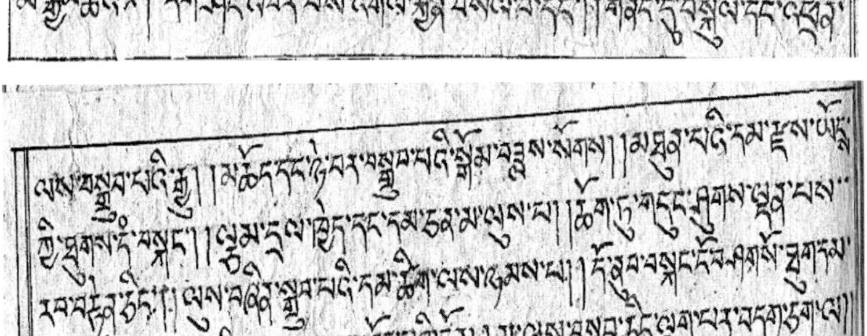

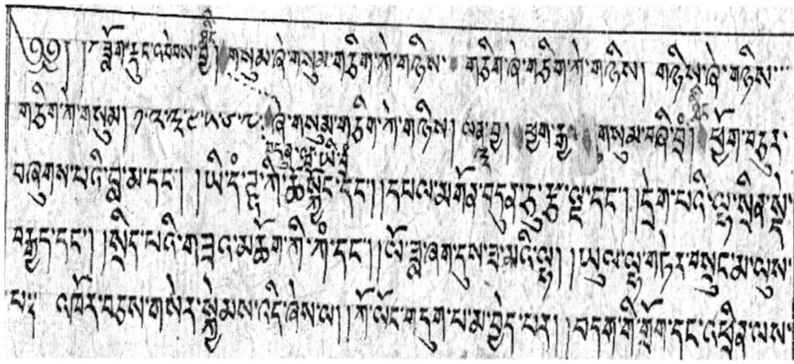

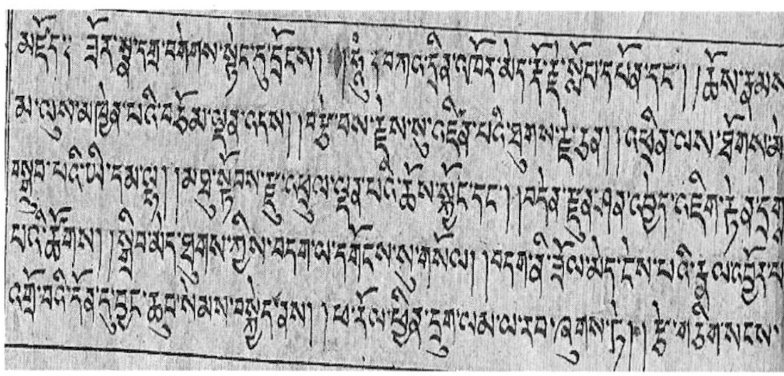

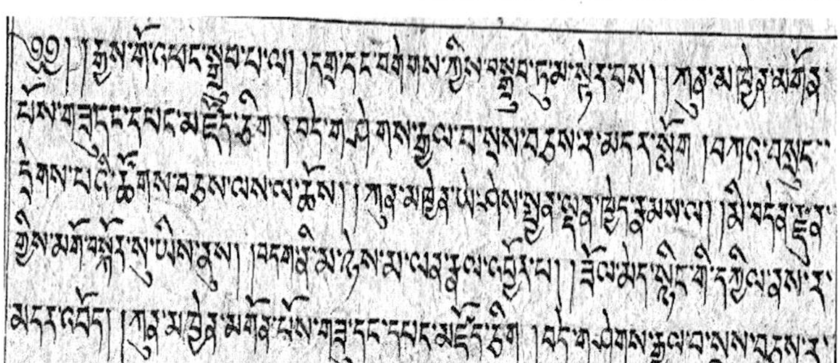

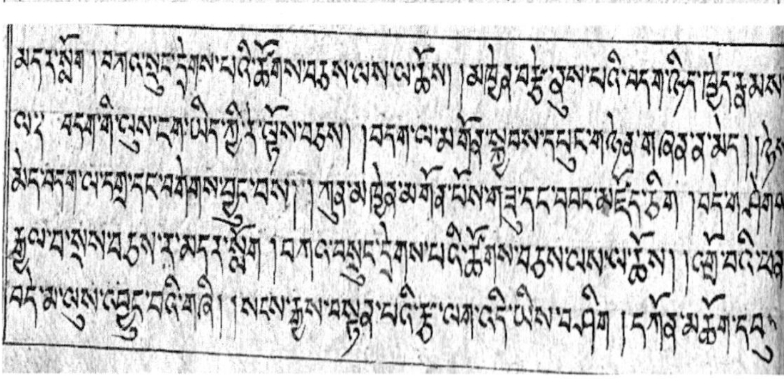

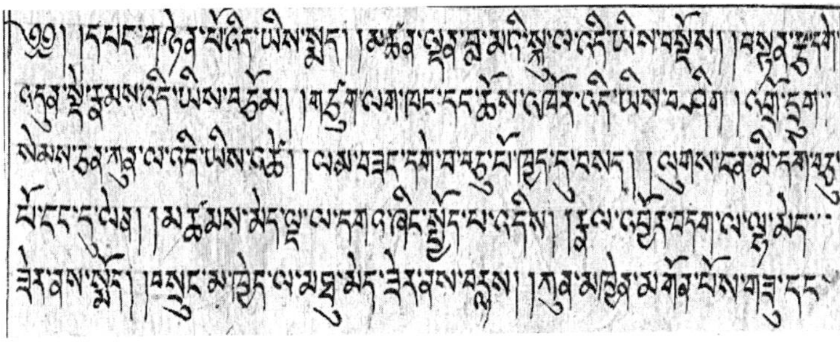
༄༅། །དཔང་གཉེན་པོའིད་ཡིས་སྐྱིད། །མཚན་ལྡན་བླ་མའི་སྐུ་ལ་འདི་ཡིས་བསྒོམས། །བསྟན་རྩ་བ
འདུན་སྒོ་རྣམས་འདི་ཡིས་བཙེམ། །གཙུག་ལག་ཁང་དང་ཆོས་འཁོར་འདི་ཡིས་བཞིག །འགྲོ་དྲུག
སེམས་ཅན་ཀུན་ལ་འདི་ཡིས་འཚེ། །ལམ་བཟང་དགེ་བ་བཅུ་པོ་ཁྲིད་དུ་བཙུད། །ལུགས་ངན་མི་དགེ་བཅུ
པོ་དང་དུ་ལེན། །མཚམས་མེད་ལྔ་ལ་དགའ་ཞིང་སྤྱོད་པ་འདིས། །རྣལ་འབྱོར་བདག་ལ་ལྷ་མེད
ཟེར་ནས་སྨོད། །བསྲུང་མ་ཁྱེད་ལ་མཐུ་མེད་ཟེར་ནས་བརླམས། །ཀུན་མཁྱེན་མགོན་པོས་གཟུ་དང

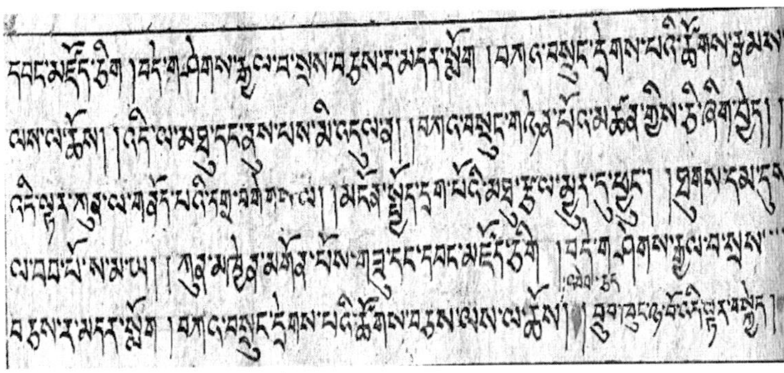
དཔང་མཛོད་ཅིག །བདག་ཞིག་རྒྱལ་བ་སྲས་བཅས་ར་མདར་སློག །བཀའ་བསྒྲུབ་རྟགས་པའི་ཚོགས་རྣམས
ལས་ལ་ཚོས། །འདི་ལ་མཐུ་དང་ནུས་པས་མི་འདུལ་ན། །བཀའ་བསྒྲུབ་གཉན་པོའི་མཚན་གྱིས་ཅི་ཞིག་བྱེད། །
འདི་ལྟར་ཀུན་ལ་གནོད་པའི་དགྲ་བགེགས་ལ། །མངོན་སྤྱོད་དྲག་པོའི་མཐུ་རྩལ་སྤྱུར་དུ་སྟོད། །ཐུགས་དམ་དུས
ལ་བབ་པོ་ས་མ་ཡ། །ཀུན་མཁྱེན་མགོན་པོས་གཟུ་དང་དཔང་མཛོད་ཅིག །བདག་ཞིག་རྒྱལ་བ་སྲས
བཅས་ར་མདར་སློག །བཀའ་བསྒྲུབ་རྟགས་པའི་ཚོགས་བཅས་ལས་ལ་ཚོས། ། ལེའུ་ཚར། །རྡུག་བྲུང་ཞྭ་མོའི་ཕྲིན་བསྐུལ། །

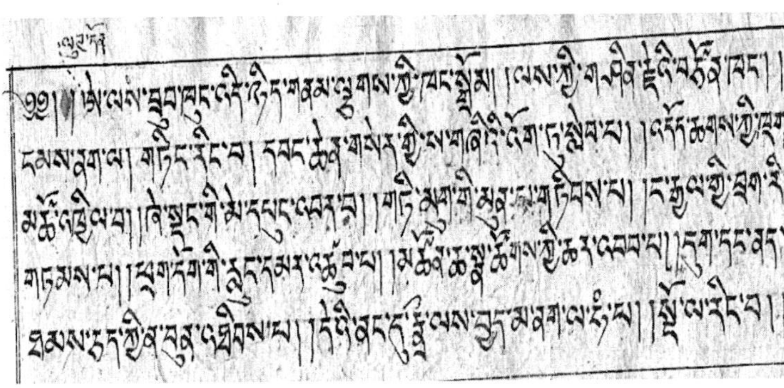
ལྷུར་དན
༄༅། །ཨོཾ་ཡེས་བྲག་ཁྲང་འདི་ཉིད་གནམ་ལྕགས་ཀྱི་ཕང་སྒྲོམ། །ཡེས་ཀྱི་ག་ཤིན་རྡོའི་བཙོན་ཁང་། །
དམས་ནག་ལ། གཉིད་རིང་བ། དབང་ཆེན་གསེར་གྱི་ས་གཞི་འོག་ཏུ་སྦེབ་པ། །འདོད་ཆགས་ཀྱི་ལྕགས
མཚོ་འཁྱིལ་བ། །ཞེ་སྡང་གི་མེ་དཔུང་འབར་བ། །གཏི་མུག་གི་མུན་ལ་གཏིབས་པ། །ང་རྒྱལ་གྱི་ནག་རི
གཏམས་པ། །ཕྲག་དོག་གི་རླུང་དམར་འཚུབ་པ། །མཆེ་ཚ་སྣ་ཚོགས་ཀྱི་ཆར་འབབ་པ། །དྲག་དང་ནད
ཐམས་ཅད་ཀྱིས་བསྣན་འཁྱིལ་བ། །དེ་ཡི་ནང་དུ་སྲི་ལས་བྱུང་མ་ནག་ལ་ཚི་པ། །སྲོ་ལ་རིང་བ། །

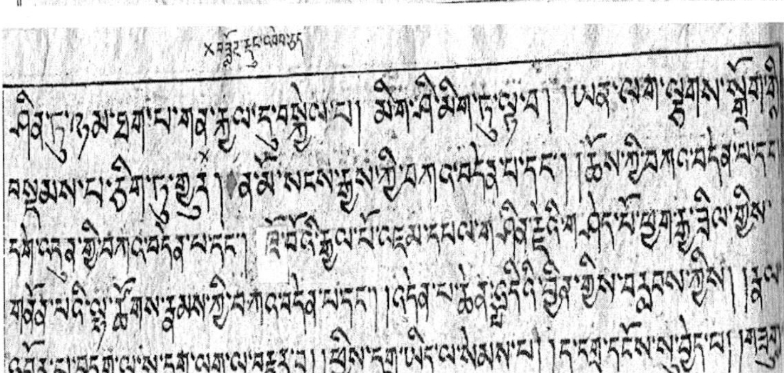
×བཟླུར་རྡུང་འབེབ་ཅན
ཤིན་ཏུ་ཉམ་ཐག་པ་གནོད་རྒྱལ་དུ་བསྐྱེལ་པ། མིག་ཤི་མིག་ཏུ་ལྟོ་བ། །ཡན་ལག་ལྟེགས་སྐྲོག་གི
བསྐྲམས་པ་ཅིག་ཏུ་སྒྲུར། །ན་མོ་སངས་རྒྱས་ཀྱི་བཀའ་བདེན་པ་དང་། །ཆོས་ཀྱི་བཀའ་བདེན་པ་དང
དགེ་འདུན་གྱི་བཀའ་བདེན་པ་དང་། །ཨོ་རྒྱན་གྱི་རྒྱལ་པོ་འཛམ་དཔལ་གཤིན་རྗེའི་གཤེད་པོ་ཕྱག་རྒྱ་ཐིལ་གྱིས
གནོན་པའི་ལྷ་ཚོགས་རྣམས་ཀྱི་བཀའ་བདེན་པ་དང་། །འཇིག་པ་ཆེན་པོ་ཡི་བྱིན་གྱིས་བརླབས་ཀྱིས། །ན་ལ
འཁོར་བ་བདག་ལ་སྡང་དགྲ་ལག་ལ་བརྫར་བ། །བྱིས་དགྲ་ཡིད་ལ་སེམས་པ། །ད་དགྲ་དངོས་སུ་བྱེད་པ། །གཟུ

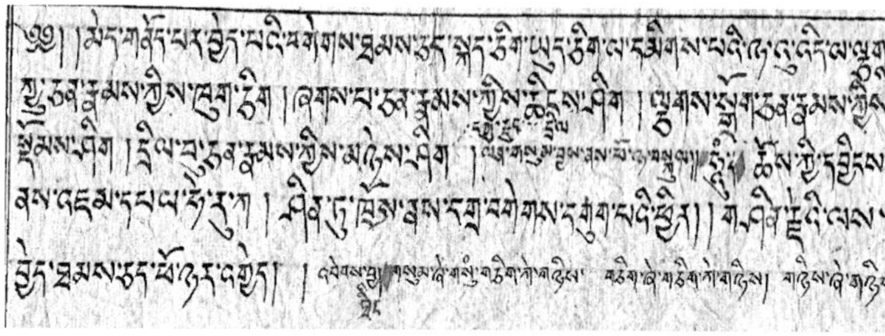

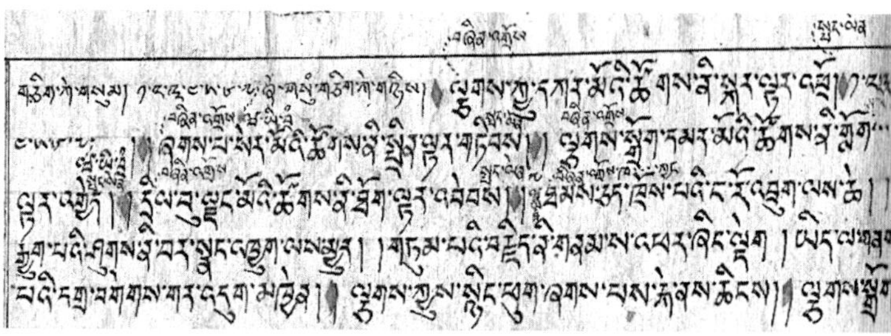

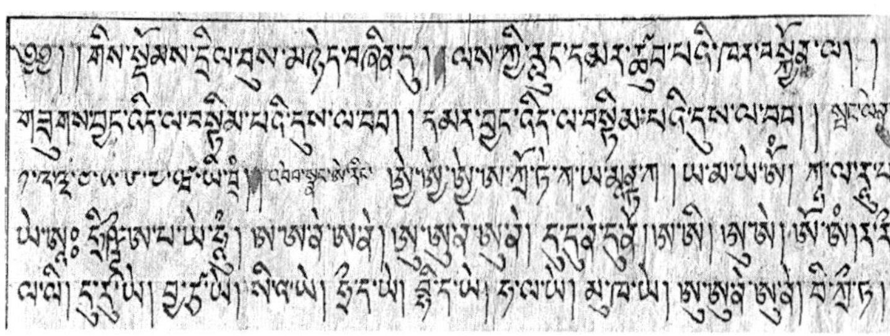

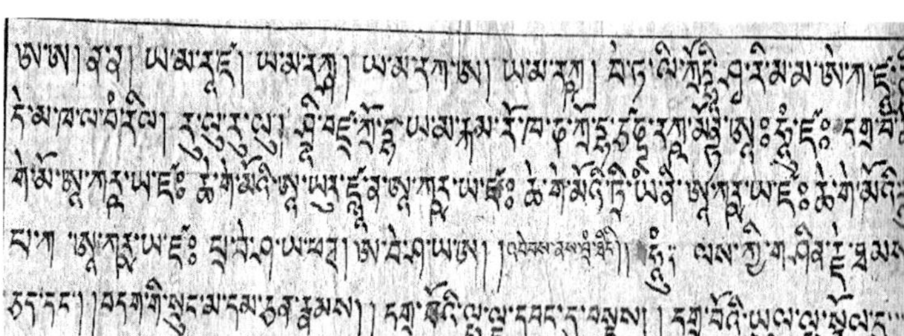

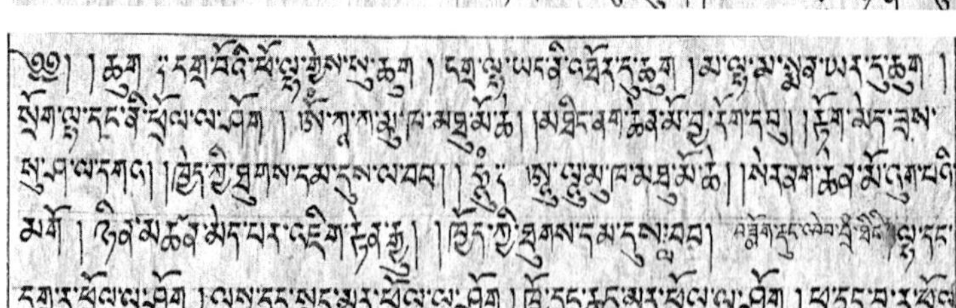

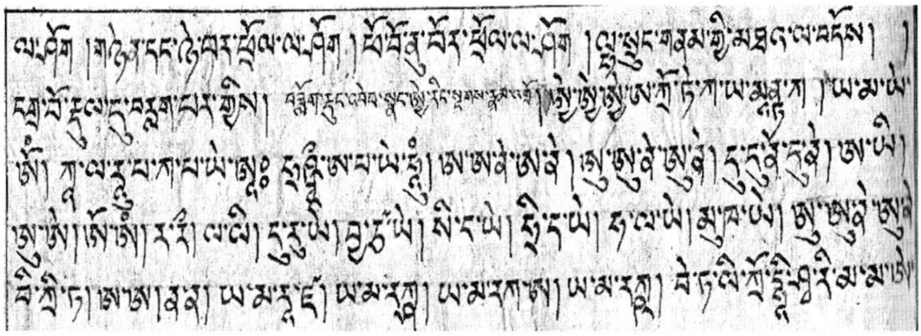

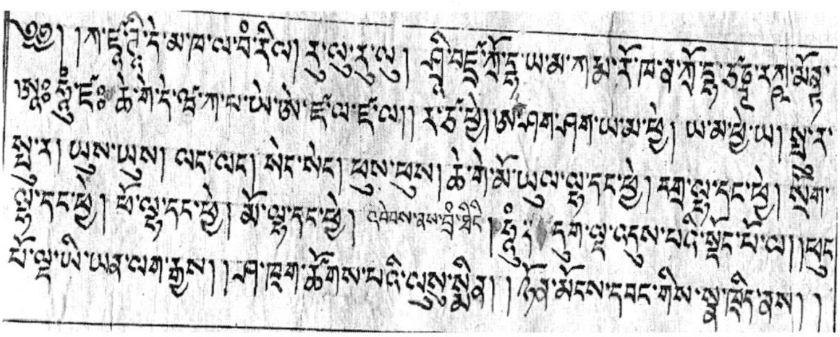

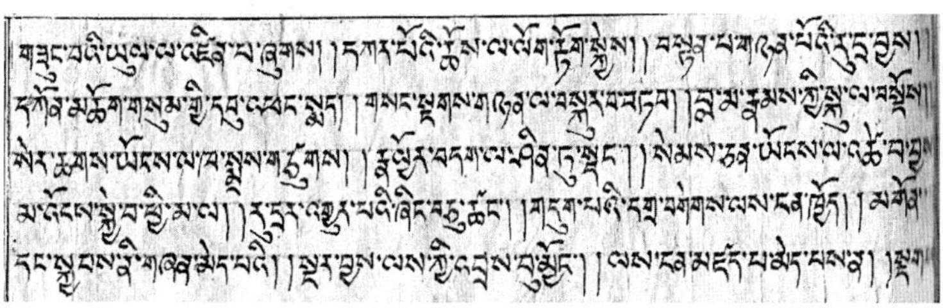

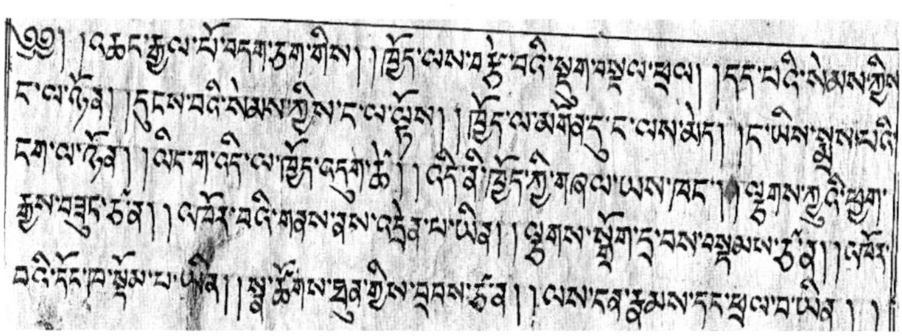

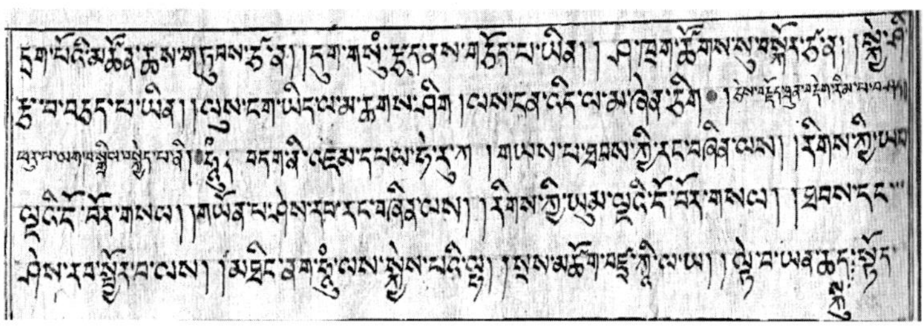

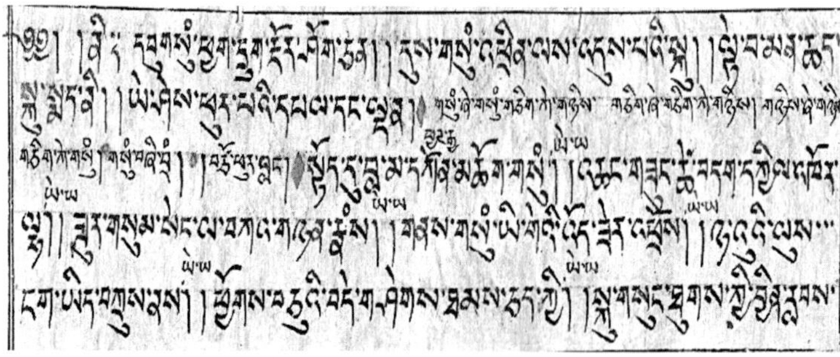

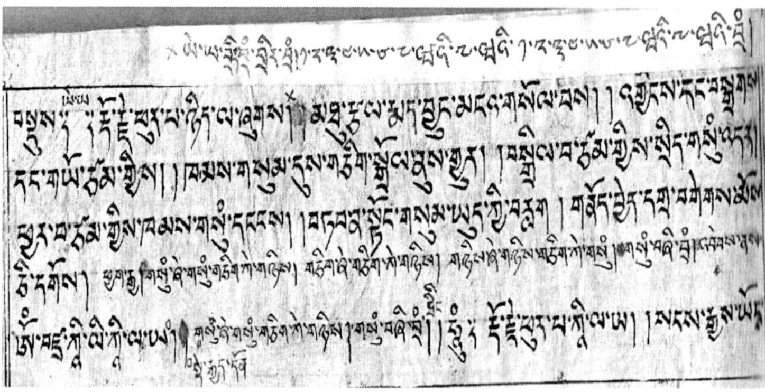

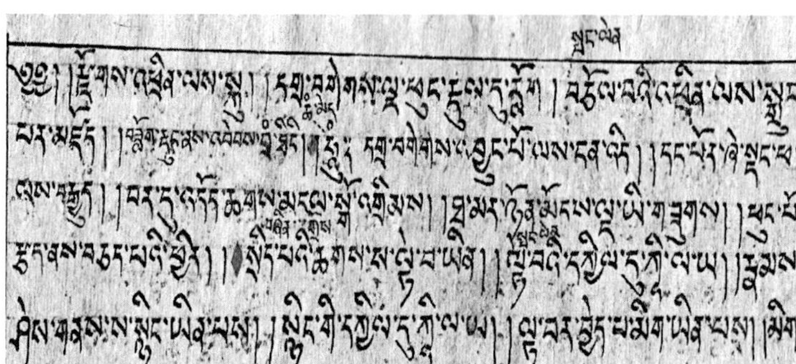

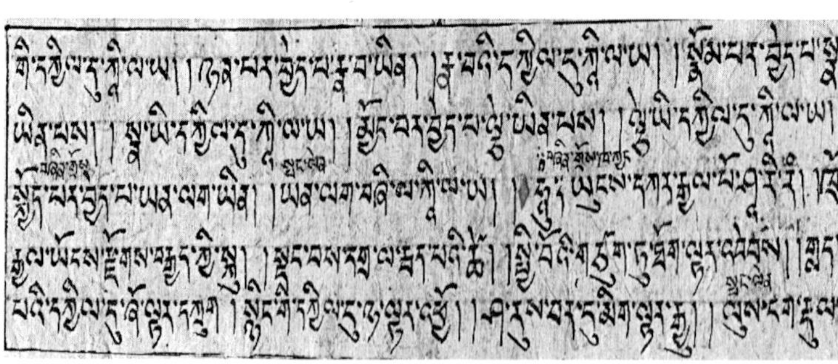

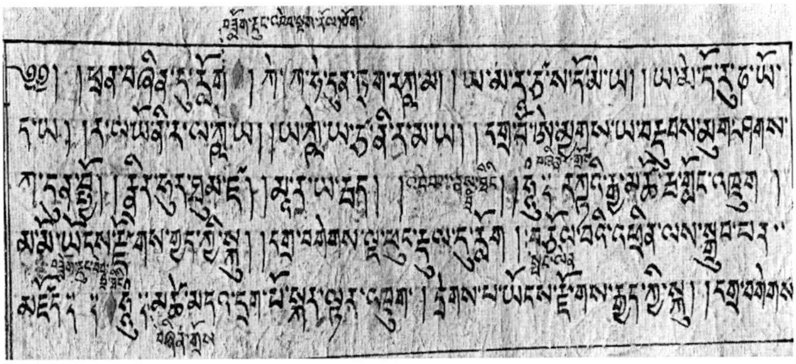

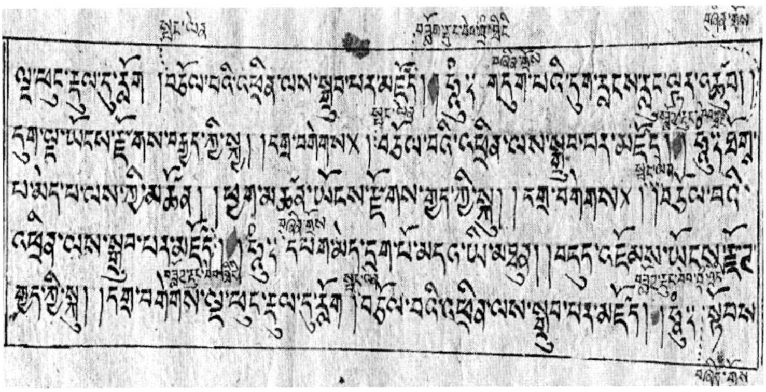

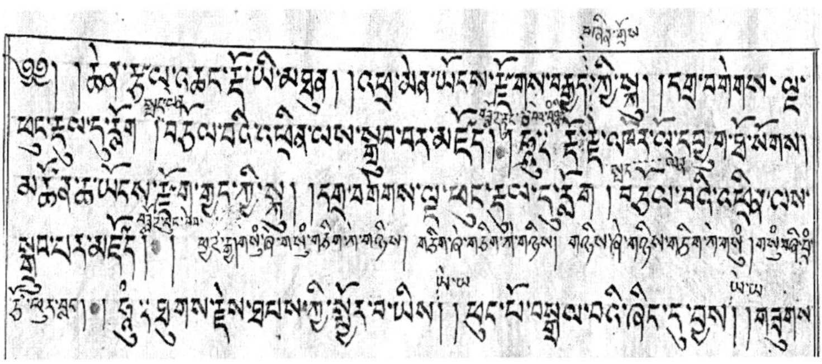

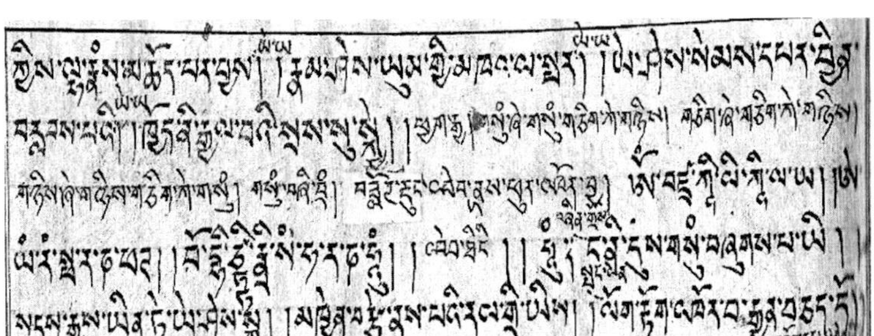

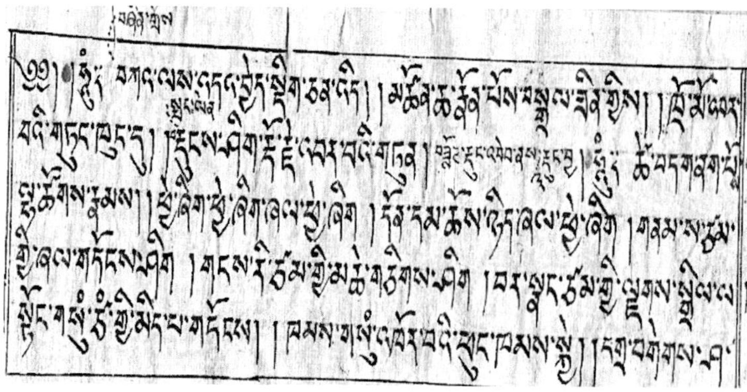

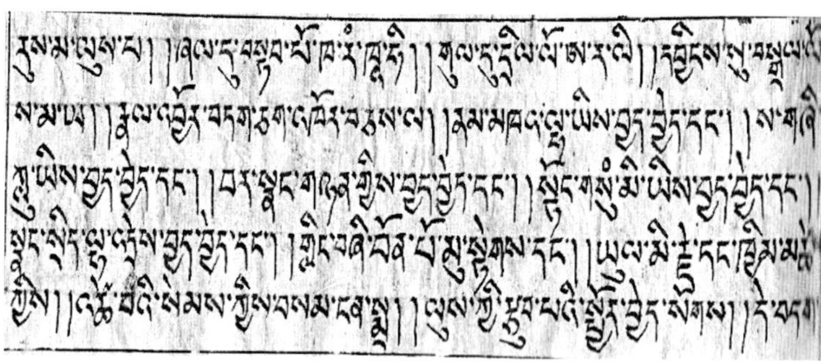

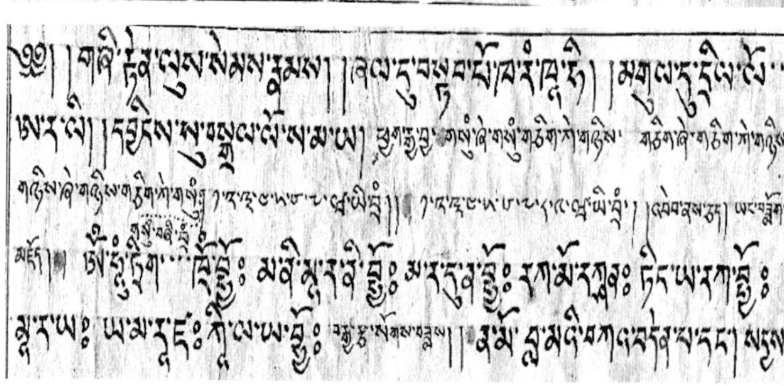

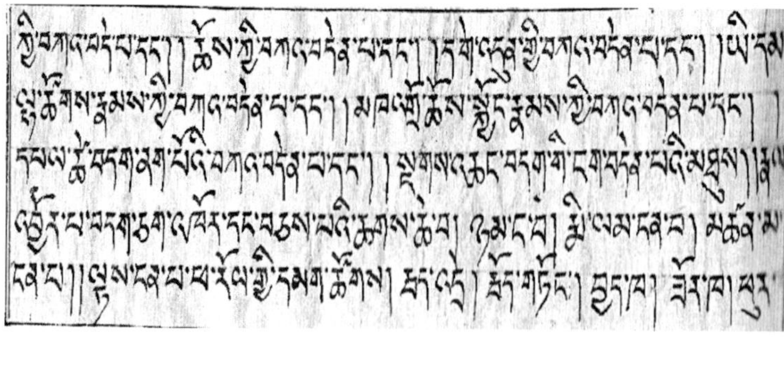

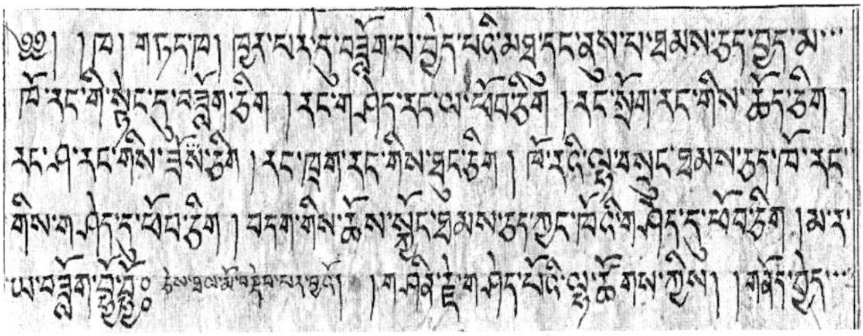

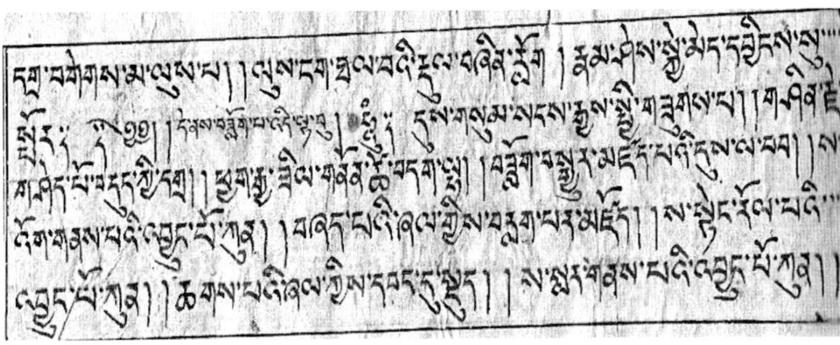

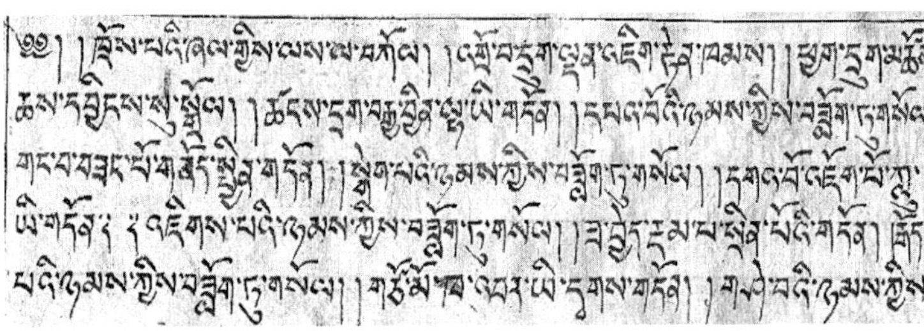

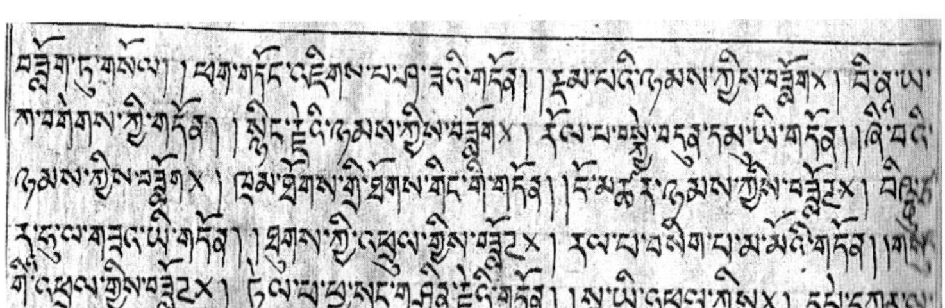

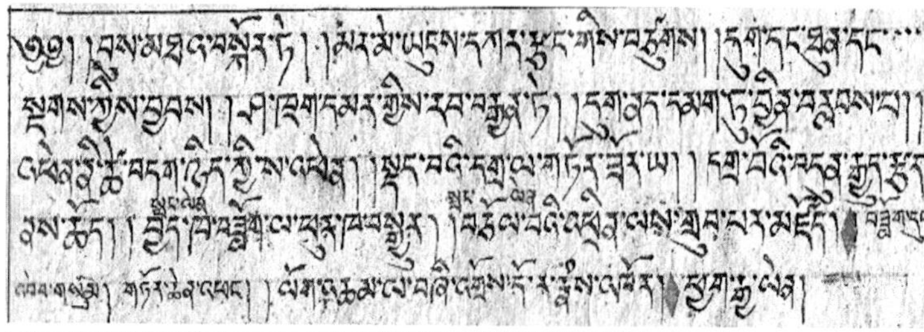

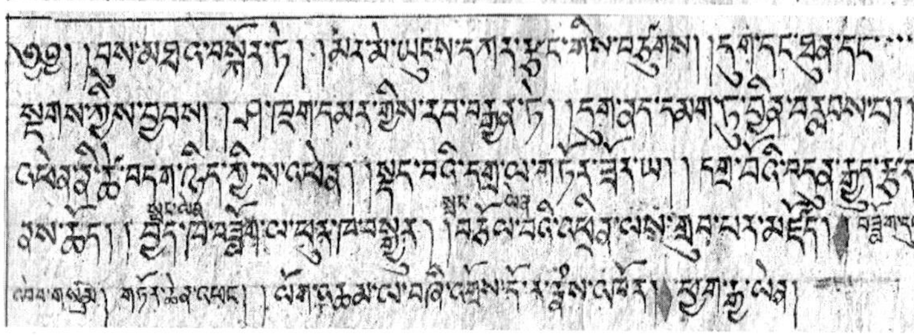

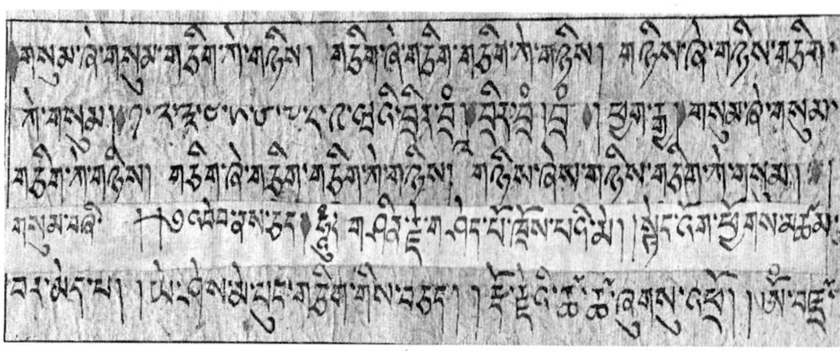

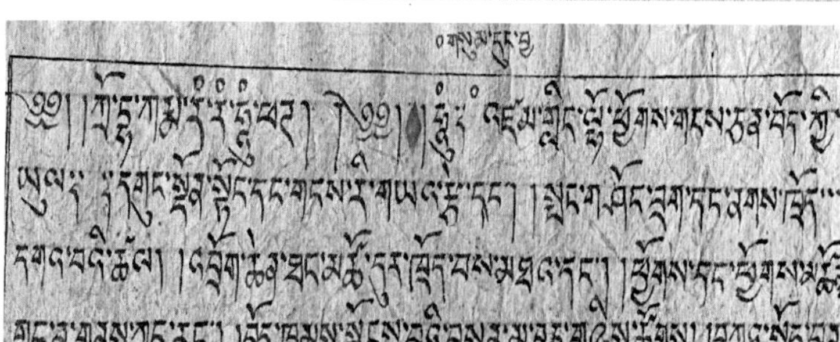

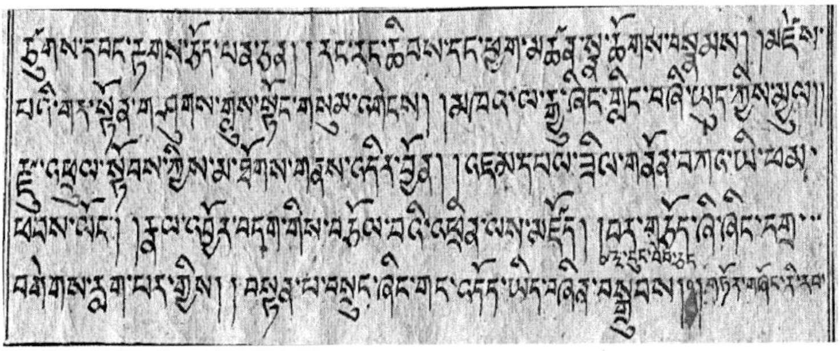

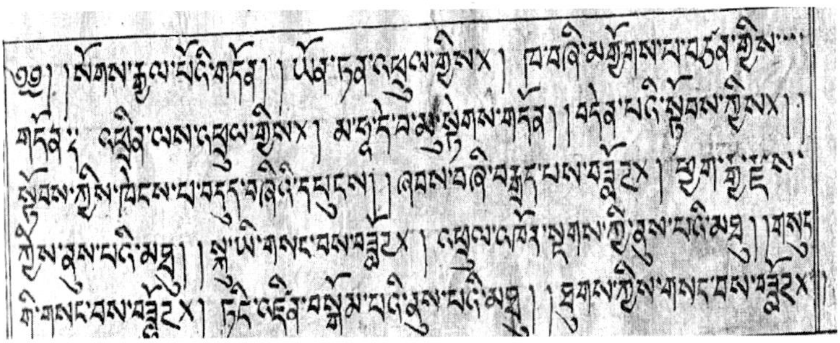

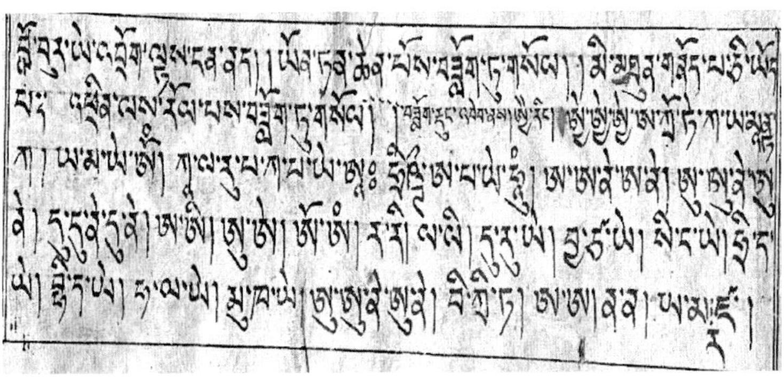

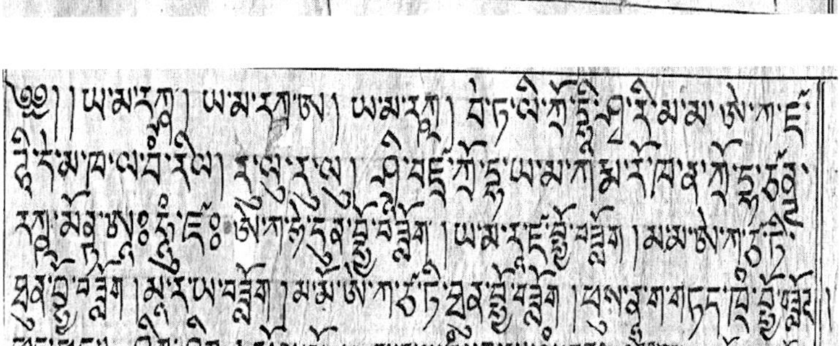

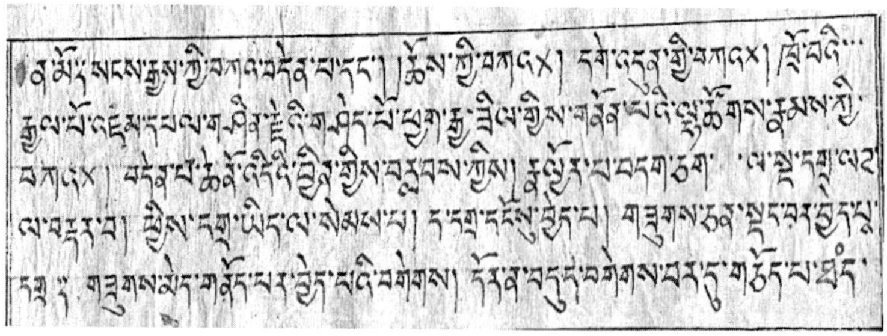

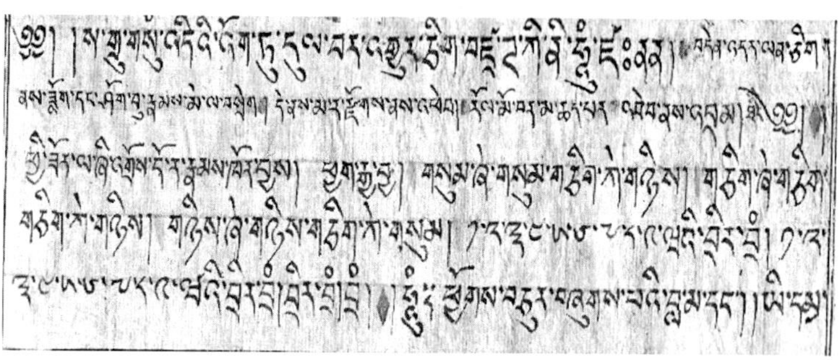

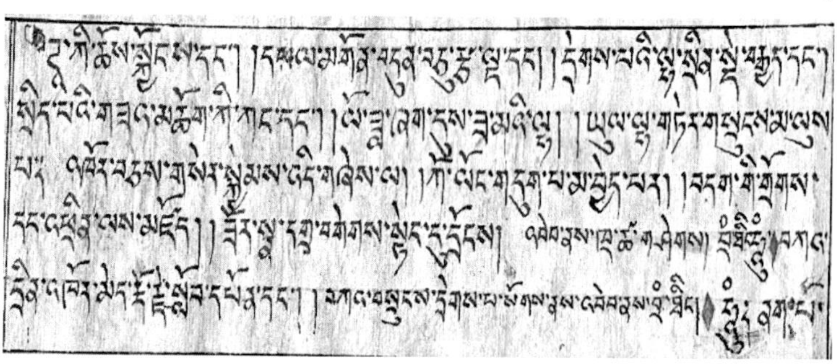

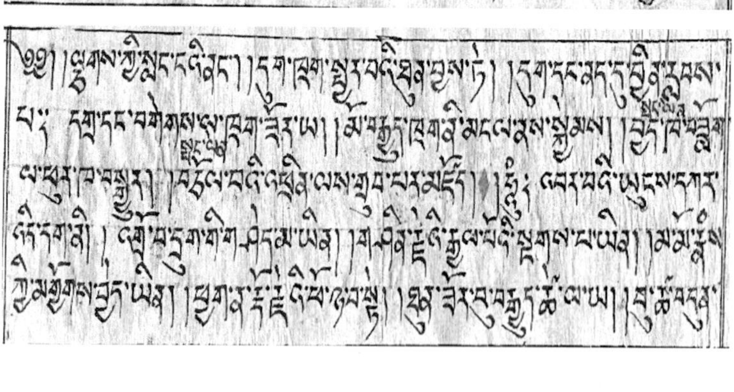

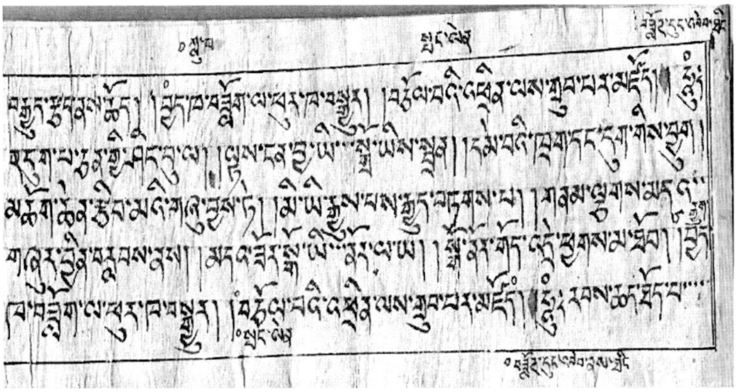

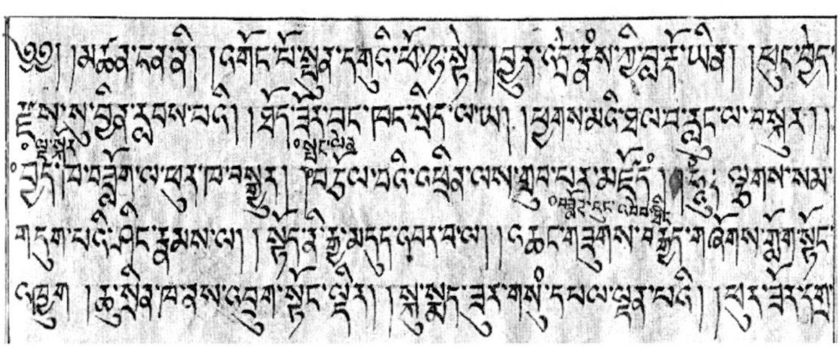

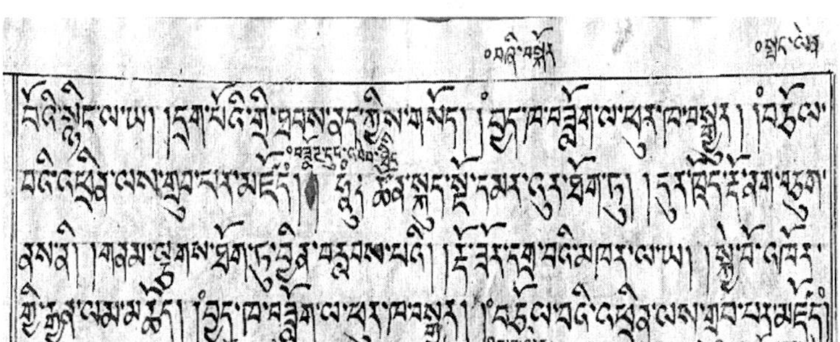

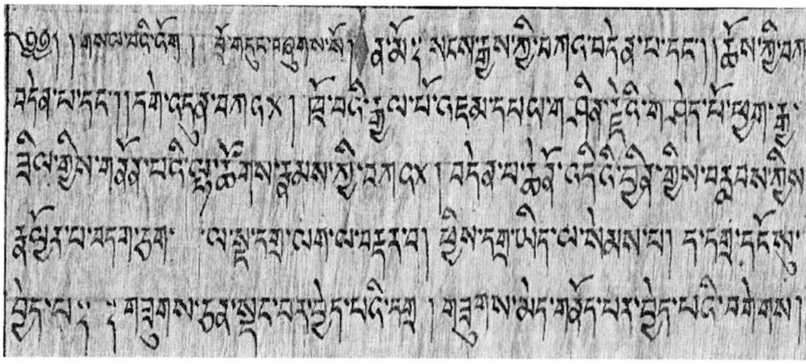

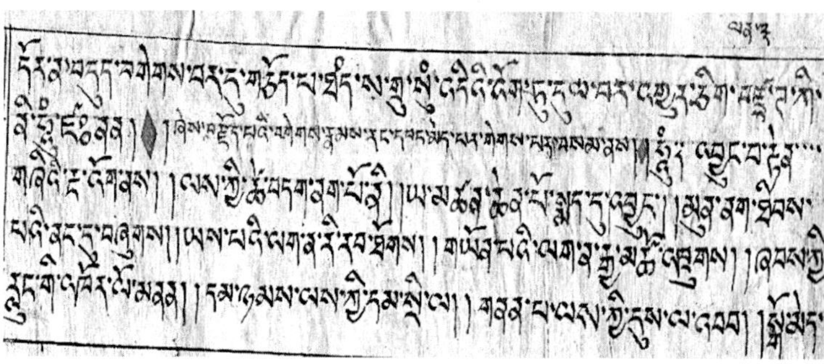

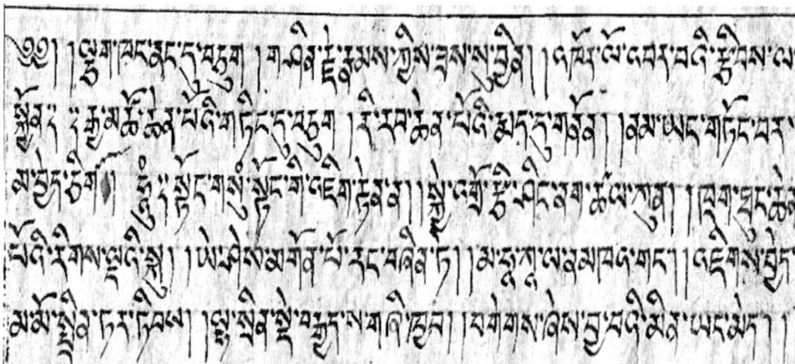

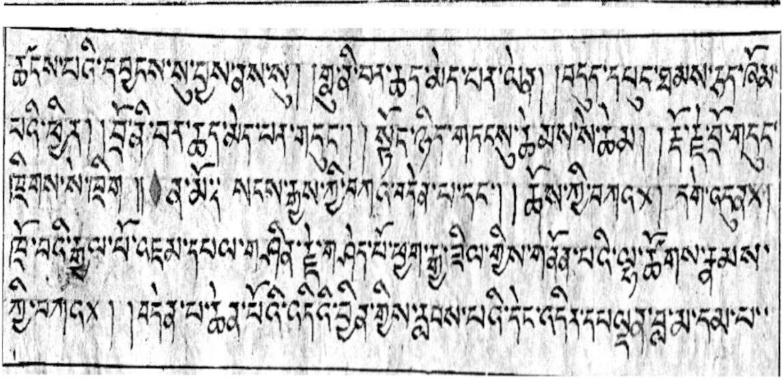

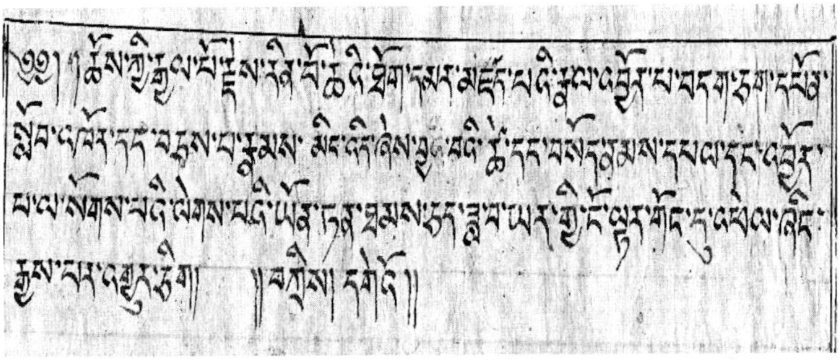

༄༅། །ཆོས་ཀྱི་རྒྱལ་པོ་རྗེ་རིན་པོ་ཆེའི་ཕྱག་དམར་མཛད་པའི་རྣལ་འབྱོར་པ་བདག་ཅག་དཔོན་སློབ་འཁོར་དང་བཅས་པ་རྣམས་ མིང་འདི་ཞེས་བྱ་བའི་ཚེ་དང་བསོད་ནམས་དཔལ་དང་འབྱོར་པ་ལ་སོགས་པའི་ལེགས་པའི་ཡོན་ཏན་ཐམས་ཅད་ཟླ་བ་ཡར་གྱི་ངོ་ལྟར་གོང་དུ་འཕེལ་ཞིང་རྒྱས་པར་འགྱུར་ཅིག། །བཀྲིས། དགེའོ།།

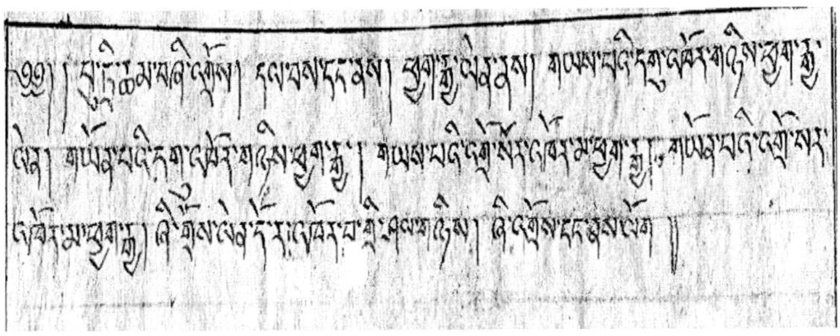

༄༅། །པུ་ཏྲི་ཚམ་པའི་འགོ་ས། དཔལ་བས་དང་ནས། ཕྱག་རྒྱ་ལེན་ནས། གཡས་པའི་དཀུ་འཁོར་གཉིས་ཕྱག་རྒྱ་ལེན། གཡོན་པའི་དཀུ་འཁོར་གཉིས་ཕྱག་རྒྱ། །གཡས་པའི་འགྲོ་སོར་འཁོར་མ་ཕྱག་རྒྱ། །གཡོན་པའི་འགྲོ་སོར་འཁོར་མ་ཕྱག་རྒྱ། ཞི་གྲུབ་ལེན་དུ་རུ་འཁོར་བ་གྲི་ཞལ་ཇུས། ཞི་འགྲོས་དང་ནས་ལེན། །

Annexure III

Rock inscriptions from Tod Valley

B.127 Inscription in rock from Hayar, Tshewang rNamgyal and the king of Kullu Parbat Singh, A.D. 1700-1730

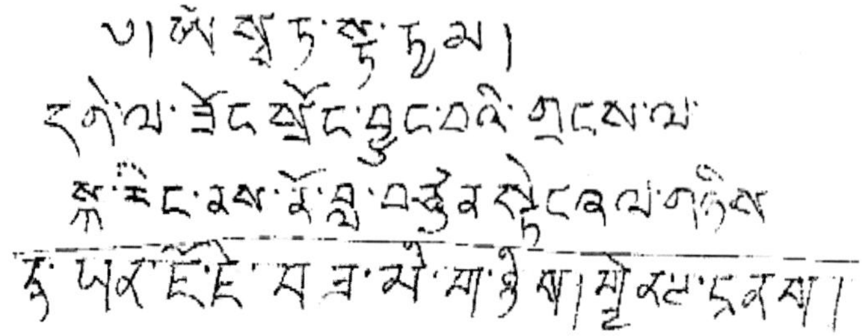

B.140 Votive inscription from village Bog, 18th -19th Century

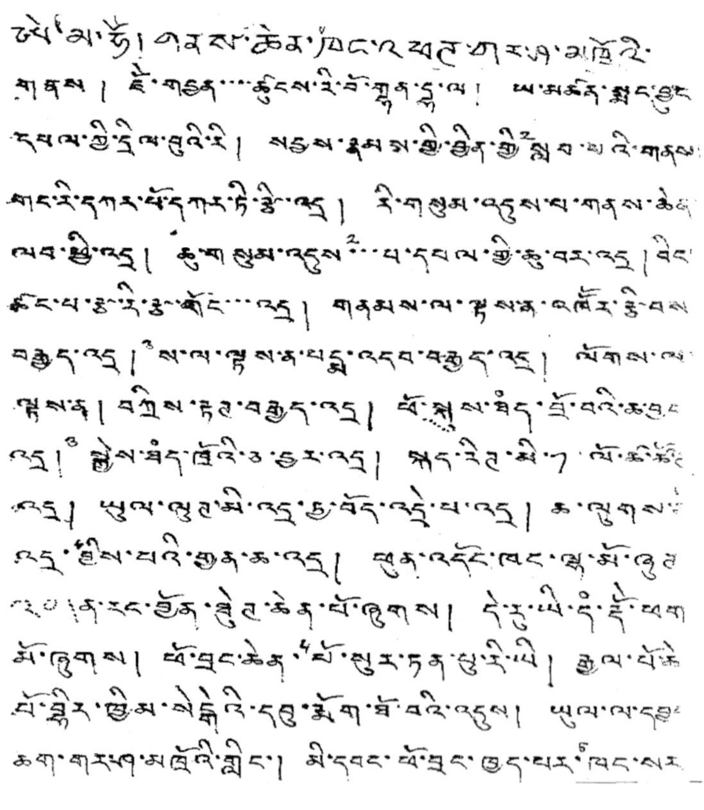

ན། དྲུ་སྒྲ་སེངྒེ་ཡུམ་སྲས་དབུ་མོག་མཐོ་ཞིང་། ཆབ་སྲིད་དར
བའི་དུས། དགེ་བཅུའི་མ་ཁྲིམས་ཀྱི་ ཡ་བོར་འབངས་འཛུ
མཛད། སྡིག་བཅུ་གཏན་ནས་བཀག་པའི་དཔལ་པོའི་
མཆོག། དེའི་མངའ་འོག་འབོག་གི་ཀཡུ་ལ་མཆོག་ན།
གཉིས། དེའི་སྲས་བཀྲ་ཤིས་བསམ་འགྲུབ་.....་དང་ནོ་འབྲུག་ཚེ་དབང་གཉིས
ཀྱི་བཙུན་མོ་བཟང་འཛིན་ཡུ་དྲོན་དང་ནོ་མོ་ལྷ་རྒྱ་གཉིས། ཡང་སྲས་བཟང་
འཛིན་ཚེ་དབང་དང་པདྨ་བུ་ཁྲིད་གཉིས།། གནང་ཚང་ཐམས་ཅད།དགེ
བའི་བསམ་པ་ཅན། དགེ་བའི་ལས་ལ་འབྲས་བུ་ར་..... 7བའོ།
སྤྱན་ཆེ་བཀོད་ནམས་བསགས་པའི་མཐུ་སྟོབས་ལས། ཆེ་འདིར་
.... སྐྱིད་མི་ཟང་ཆར་བབ་ཅིང་། ཕྱི་མའི་དོན་དུ་8དགེ་བ་དཔག་..
མེད་མཛད། ཁྱད་པར་ཡིག་དྲུག་སྙིང་རྩ་ཅན་ གཅིག་དང་བརྒྱ་
གཅིག་བཞེངས། མར་རྒྱུད་མཐའ་མེད་འགྲོ་བ་ཡོ....8ལ་ཀྱི
དོན་དུ་ཐུབ་བསམ་རྣམ་པར་དག་པའི་མཡོ་ནས་མཛད་པ་
ང་མཆར་ཆེ་ཆེ ॥

B.135 Inscription on a mani at Khangsar

........རྒྱལ་པོ་
སྟུ་རཾ་སྣར་སྤྱར། རྒྱལ་སྲས་དམ་པ་སྒྲ་ཉིམ་སེང་གི་དབུ་
མོག་ཐོ་ ... ཆབ་སྲིད་རྒྱས་འགྱུར་ཅིག།......

B.140 Votive inscription from village Bog, 18th -19th Century

ཨོཾ་ཨཱ་ཧཱུྃ། ཕ་ནས་ཆེན་ཁང་འབང་ཀ་ར་ཤ་མཁའི་
ཀ་ནས། རྗེ་གཙན་...སྟོངས་རི་བོ་རྣམ་དྲུ་ལ། ཡ་མཆོད་སྣང་གྲུང
དཔལ་ཀྱི་དྲི་ལ་བུའི་རི། སྡེས་རྣམ་ས་ཀྱི་ཀྱིན་ཀྱི་སྐྱ་བ་པའི་གནས་
སང་རི་དཀར་པོད་ཀར་ཏི་རྩེ་འདུ། རི་ག་སུམ་འདུས་པ་གནས་ཆེན
ལབ་ཀྱི་འདུ། རྒྱ་གསུམ་འདུས་...པ་དཔལ་ཀྱི་རྒྱུ་བར་འདུ། ཞིང
སྐྱོང་པ་ཙ་རི་ཙ་གོང་...འདུ། གནམ་ས་ལ་རྣ་ལན་འཁོར་རྩེ་བས
བརྒྱད་འདུ། ས་ལ་ལྷ་ས་ན་པདྨ་འདབ་བརྒྱད་འདུ། ལོག་ས་ལ
ལྷ་ས་ན། འཁྲིས་རྟ་བརྒྱད་འདུ། ཕོ་སྐྱལ་ཐིད་བྲོ་བའི་ཆ་བ
འདུ། སྐྱེལ་ཐིད་བྲེའི་ཅ་ཅར་འདུ། སྐད་རིའ་མི་ཀ་ ལོ་ཙ་རྩེ
འདུ། ཡུལ་ལུའ་མི་འདུ་རྒྱ་བོད་འདྲེ་པ་འདུ། ཆ་ལུག་ལ
འདུ་ཁྲིལ་པའི་རྒྱན་ཆ་འདུ། ལུན་འདོད་ཁང་ལྷ་མོ་ཞུའ
...ན་རང་ཅན་རྒྱུའ་ཆེན་པོ་ཞུགས། དེ་རྩ་ཡི་དྲི་རྗེ་ཕག
མོ་ཞུགས། ཕོ་བྲང་ཆེན་པོ་ཤུར་ཏན་ཤུ་རི་ཡི། རྒྱལ་པོ་ཆེ
པོ་བླེར་ཁྲིམ་ལེགས་ཀྱི་དབུ་སྨོག་བོ་བའི་འདུས། ཡུལ་ལ་དབྱེ
ཆག་གཡས་མཁྲེའི་གླིང་། མི་དབང་ཕོ་བྲང་ཁྱད་པར་ཁང་ལར

ན། ནྲྀ་སུ་སེངགེ་ཡུམ་སྲས་དབུ་མོག་མཐོ་ཞིང་། ཆབ་སྲིད་དར
བའི་དུས། དགེ་བཅུའི་མ་ཁྲིམས་ཀྱི་[6] ཕ་བོར་འབངས་འཛུམ
མཛད། སྡིག་བཅུ་གཏན་ནས་བཀག་པའི་དཔལ་པོའི་
མཆོག། དེའི་མངའ་འོག་འབོག་གི་གཡུ་ལ་མཆོག་ན།
གཉིས། དེའི་སྲས་བཀྲ་ཤིས་བསམ་འགྲུབ་....[6]་དང་ནོ་ཞུགས་ཚེ་དབང་གཉིས

ཀྱི་བརྟན་མོ་བསྟན་འཛིན་ཕུ་ཐྲིད་དང་ནོ་མོ་ཨ་ཆུ་གཉིས། ཡང་སྲས་བསྟན་
འཛིན་ཚེ་[7]དབང་དང་བཀྲ་ཕུ་ཐྲིད་གཉིས།། གཞན་ཚང་ཐམས་ཅད།དགེ
བའི་བསམ་པ་ཅན། དགེ་བའི་ལས་ལ་འབྲས་བུ་ར་.....[7]བའོ།
སྟོན་ཆོ་བཀོད་ནམས་བསགས་པའི་མཐུ་སྟོབས་ལས། ཚེ་འདིར་
.... གྱིད་མི་ཟང་ཆར་བབ་ཅིང་། ཕྱི་མའི་དོན་དུ་[8]དགེ་བ་དཔག་..
མེད་མཛད། ཁྱད་པར་ཡི་གེ་དྲུག་སྟོང་ར་ཅན་གཅིག་དང་བརྒྱ་
གཅིག་བཞེངས། མར་རྒྱུད་མཐའ་མེད་འགྲོ་བ་ཡོ....[8]ས་ཀྱི
དོན་དུ་ཐུག་བསམ་རྣམ་པར་དག་པའི་མགོ་ནས་མཛད་པ་
ངོ་མཚར་ཆེ་ཆེ ॥

B.141 Votive Inscription on Mani stone, Bog, referring Dharam Singh, (1770-1810) (Bhoti language and script)

ལ་རྒྱན། ཐུགས་རྗེ་སྤྱན་གྱི་འགྲོ་ལ་གཟིགས། མགོན་
པོ་སྤྱན་རས་གཟིགས་ལ་ཕྱག་འཚལ་ལོ॥ ॥ ཨོཾ་མ་ཎི།
དེ་ནས་གང་ཏི་ཤིའི་རྒྱང་གི་ལྷོ་ཕྱོགས་སུ། ས་གཞི་ལ...
ཁྱིན་ཆགས་ལྷོའི་འཛམ་བུ་གླིང་སེངྒེ་ཁ་བབ།ཀྱི་མ་སེངྒེ
དབུ་མོག་མཐོ་བའི་དུས། ཡུལ་ལ་དབང་ཆགས་རྒྱ་གར་
ཁང་ལས་རྒྱར། མ་དཔང་ཆབ་བ་རྣམས་སྐྱོང་དབུ་མཐོག་ཐ་བའི་དུས། ཡུལ་
ལ་དགེ་བཅུ་རྗེས་སྲུ་འབོག་འདིར། མིང་གིས་ཁྱུང་བརྟན་ཀྱིན་སིང་..
པའི་རྒྱུད་ལྷུན་་སྒྲུབ་[3]...འི་མཆོག་རྒྱུར་ཆོ་ཁྱུངས་ཆེས་ཤིད
དང་། ཨ་མ་སོ་ནམས་དང་། ཨ་ཚོ་དངོས་གྲུབ་དང་། ནོ་དོན...
གྲུབ་དང་། ནོ་མོ་བཟང་མོ་དང་། .... དཔོན་ཆེན་
འཕགས་པ་ཆོས་འཕེལ་དང་། ཆོས་འབྱོར་དང་། རྡོ་རྗེ་རྒྱལ་པོ་དང་།
ལག་པ་ཤེས་ཚེ་དབྱ....[4]....མ་གན་རྫོམ་དང་། བུའི་མཆོག་
རྒྱུར་བཀྲིས་བསོད་འབྱོར་དང་། བསྟན་འཛིན་ཕུ་ཐྲིད་དང་།ཚེ
བའི་མཆོག་རྒྱུར་ཆེ་དབྱངས་བསྟན་འཛིན་དང་། ཚེ་ཆོས་...
མཆོག་རྒྱུར་པདྨ་ཕུ་ཐྲིད་དང་། དགེ་རྒྱས་ལ་ལངས་སོལ
ཛ་ཉ་གཉིས་རྗེ་དོན་ཤིང་ཨ་རག་ [5]རྒྱང། ཆེ་དབྱངས།

དེན་ཚེ་ནས་ཡ་རག་དང་ལག་པ་བརྒྱང་། དོམ་བྱ་ཚེ་རིང་
ནས་ལང་མ་དོན་ཤིང་ཚེ་བྱུང་། སྐྱེ་ནས་ལག་པ་ཚེ་རྒྱུན
རྗེན་མ་ཁེ་ཐུན་རྒྱུ་དང་ཇེ་བ་ཡོད། ཁང་ཆུང་མཆོད་རྗེན་བ
ཡོད།

Bibliography

Ahir, D.C. (1993), *Himalayan Buddhism:Past and Present*, Delhi.

Charles Horne (1871), 'Notes on an Ancient Indian Vase, with an Account of the Engravings thereupon', in *The Journal of the Royal Asiatic Society of Great Britain and Ireland*, New Series, Vol. 5, (367-375).

Cunningham, Alexander (1854), *Ladak, Physical, Statistical and Historical*, reprinted, 1970, New Delhi.

Dorje, C. (1997), 'Conservation of Ardhanarisvara Temple, Mandi, Himachal Pradesh" in *Facets of Indian Civilization-Recent Perspective - Essays in honour of Prof. B.B. Lal*, Vol.III, New Delhi, pp.676-79; -do- (2006), 'Pangi Valley- A Brief note on Archaeological Exploration' in *Kunzom*, January-December 2006, pp.64-66; Dorje, C. (2008), 'Mirkula Devi Temple, Udaipur-Conservation measures' in *Kunzom*, Part 3-4. January-December, 2007-2008; -do- (2009),' Mirkula Devi Temple, Udaipur in Lahoul & Spiti (HP)' in *Kaladharpana The Mirror of Indian Art-Essays in the Memory of Shri Krishna Deva*, ed. Devangna Desai & Arundhati Banerji, Delhi; -do- (2014) 'Note on Conservation Problems in Monuments located in Spiti with special reference to Buddhist Monasteries at Tabo in Himchal Pradesh' in *Manimahesh-A Journal of Himalayan Studies*, Vol.V, December,pp.32-35; -d- (2013) *Monumental Heritage of Pangi*, New Delhi.

Dorje, C. & A. Jha (1994) 'A Winter Trail' in *The India Magazine*,January, pp.6-15, Mumbai.

Errington, Elizabeth & Joe Cribb (Ed.). (2012). 'Vase with Incised scenes', in The Crossroads of Asia: Transformation in Image & Symbol, The Ancient Indie & Iran Trust, Cambridge' pp. 163-164.

Francke, A.H. (1914), *Antiquities of Indian Tibe*t. In 2parts,. Archaeological Survey of India, reprinted, New Delhi, 1994; -do- (1906), F*irst Collection of Tibetan Historical Inscriptions on Rock and Stone from Western Tibet*, Kyelang; -do- (1907), *Second Collection of Tibetan Historical Inscriptions on Rock and Stone from Western Tibet*, Kyelang; -do- (1907) *Saint Mark in Tinan*, Kyelang; -do- *List of Ancient Monuments Lahul &Spiti*, Archaeological Survey, Panjab and United Provinces

Circle, unpublished; -do- (1907), *Die historischen und mythologischen Erinnerungen der Louler*, Kyelang; -do- (1907), *A History of Western Tibet, One of the Unknown Empires*, rep., New Delhi, 1977. -do- (1906 & 1907) 'Archaeology in Western Tibet', in *Indian Antiquary*, vol. xxxv and xxxvi; -do- (1907) '*History of Lahaul* (unpublished).

Garsha. (2011) *Garsha. Heart land of the Dakinis: a mirror into Lahaul sacred time and space*. Keylong: Young Drukpa Association Garsha (Lahaul).

Gazetteers. (1917*). Kangra District Gazetteers, Lahul Spiti. (Kangra District. Parts III, IV*. Vol. XXX A), Shimla Reprinted, 2003.

-do-(1898). *Gazetteer of the Kangra District Parts II to IV, Kullu, Lahul and Spiti* 1897, reprinted, New Delhi 1994.

Handa, O. C. 2001 *Buddhist Western Himalaya*: *A Politico-religious History*. New Delhi.

Harcourt AFP (1972) *The Himalayan Districts of Kooloo, Lahoul and Spiti*. New Delhi.

Hutchinson J, Vogel J.Ph. (1933) *History of the Panjab Hill States*. Vol 1-2. Lahore, reprinted 1994.

Khosla, Romi (1979) *Buddhist Monasteries in the Western Himalayas*, Kathmandu.

Klimburg-Salter D (1994) 'Tucci Himalayan Archives Report, 2: The 1991 Expedition to Himachal Pradesh'. *East and West*, Vol. 44-No.1 (March 1994); -do- (1982), 'Introduction: The Art of the Western Himalaya in Historical Perspective', in *The Silk Route and the Diamond Path: Esoteric Buddhist Art on the Trans-Himalayan Trade Routes*. Los Angeles: UCLA.

Luczanits, Christian (2004), Buddhist Sculpture in Clay, Serindia Publications, Chicago; -do- (1994), 'Another Rin chen bzang po Temple?' in *East and West,* Vol. 44-No.1, (March 1994); -do-(2014), 'From Kashmir to Western Tibet: The Many Faces of a Regional Style.' in *Collecting Paradise. Buddhist Art of Kashmir and Its Legacies*, edited by Rob Linrothe. New York & Evanston: Rubin Museum of Art and Mary & Leigh Block Museum of Art, Northwestern University, pp. 108-149.

Maxwell, T.S. (1980), 'Lākhamaṇḍal and Trilokināth. The Transformed Functions of Hindu Architecture in Two Cross-Cultural Zones of the Western Himalaya', in *Art International*, 24.1—2 (1980), 9—74 (p. 9).

Moorcroft, W. & George Trebeck (1841) *Travels in the Himalayan Provinces of Hindustan and the Panjab; in Ladakh and Kashmir; in Peshawar, Kabul, Kunduz, and Bokhara. From 1819 to 1825.*

Nebesky-Wojkowitz, Rene de. (1976). Tibetan Religious Dances, Mouton, The Hague; -do-(1956*) Oracles and Demons of Tibet. The Cult and Iconography of the Tibetan Protective Deities*, The Hague.

N. Devy and Tobdan ed. (2017) *'the Languages of Himachal Pradesh' Vol.11, Part 2 (PLSI) (People's Linguistic Survey of India)*, Delhi.

Noci, Francesco (1994), 'Observations on the Architecture and on a Carved Wooden Door of the Temple of Mirkula Devi at Udaipur, Himachal Pradesh' *East and West*, Vol. 44-No.1, (March 1994).

Roerich, George De. (1934). 'The Tibetan Dialects of Lahul', in Tibetica I, *Journal of Urusvati Himalayan Research Institute*, Vol. III, of the Roerich Museum, Naggar and New York. (83-189).

Rose, H. A. (1919) 1990. *Glossary of the tribes and castes of the Punjab and the North West Frontier Province*. Vols. 1-3. Rep. New Delhi, 1990.

Sahni, R.N. (1994) *Lahoul, the Mystery Land in the Himalayas*, New Delhi.

Sankrityayan, Rahul. (1948). *Tibbat me bauddh dharma*, second edition, 1979, Kitab Mahal, Illahabad.

Schubert J (1935). 'Der tibetische Māhātmya des Wallfahrtsplatzes Trilokināth', in *Artibus Asiae*, Vol. 5 (2-4), 76-78, 127-136.

Schweirger, Peter (1996) 'STtag-Ttsang Ras-pa's Exceptional Life as Pilgrims'in *Kailash: A Journal of Himalayn Studies*, Vol.XVIII, No.1-2,pp.81-108.

Shuttleworth, H.Lee. (1922). 'Border Countries of the Punjab Himalaya', in *The Geographical Journal*, Vol. LX, No. 4, (pp. 242-264); -do- (1923). A Wool Mart of the Indo-Tibetan Borderland, *Geographical Review*, Vol. 13, No. 4, Oct. 1923, (pp. 552-558).

Singh Gill, Manohar. (2010). *Himalayan Wonderland: Travels in Lahaul and Spiti*. New Delhi.

Singh, Madanjeet (1968). *Himalayan Art,Wall Painting and Sculpture in Ladakh, Lahaul and Spiti, the Siwalik Ranges, Nepal, Sikkim and Bhutan*, London.

Snellgrove, D.L. (1957). *Buddhist Himalaya*, Philosophical Library, New York,

Stutchbury E (1991) *Rediscovering Western Tibet. Gonpa, Chorten and the Continuity of Practice with a Tibetan Community in the Indian Himalaya*. PhD Thesis, Canberra; -do-(1994) 'Perception of landscape in Karzha: Sacred Geography and the Tibetan system of Geomancy', in *The Tibet Journal*, 19 (4), pp. 59-102.

sTag-Tshang Ras-pa, (ah): *au-rgyan mkha'-'gro'i gling-gi lam-yig thar-lam bgrod-pa'i them-skas*, Hemis, Ladakh.

Tashi Dawa. (1994). 'Chandra and Bhaga', in *Popular Antiquities, Mountains and Rivers, ed. Gurmukh Singh Bedi*, Atma Ram & Sons, Delhi.

Thakur, Laxman S. (1997), 'Tibetan Historical Inscriptions from Kinnaur and Lahaul-Spiti: A Survey of Recent Discoveries" in *Proceedings of the 7th Seminar of the IATS*, Vienna, Vol.II, pp.967-79; -do- (1999) *Buddhism in the Western Himalaya: A Study of Tabo Monastery*, Delhi.

Tobdan (1984) *History & Religions of Lahul: From the Earliest of Circa A.D. 1950*, Delhi; -do- (1979) 'La-ra — Lahul ke devataon ki kahani',in *Somsi*, July 1979, Shimla, pp.52-61; -do- (1989) 'Namthar Literature in Tibet and India' in *Journal Asiatic Society Bengal*, Vol. XXXI, No. 3-4, Kolkutta, ppo 95-109; -do- (1990) *Bhoti Parichaya-Vyakaran evam Anuvad*, Tinno Lahul; -do- (1992) 'Spiti-A Historical Survey' in *Himalya Past and Present*, 1991-92, Vol.II, Almora, pp.303-318; -do- (2000) *Kullu A Study In History-From the Earliest to AD 1900*, Delhi; -do- (2008)'The Canda-Kinnara Jataka, and the Kinnara and the Canda Parvata', in *Expressions in Indian Art* (Essays in Memory of Sh. M.C. Joshi), II vols., 2008, edited by B.R. Mani and Alok Tripathi, Agam Prakashan, New Delhi, (459-464); do-(2008*) Cultural History of Western Trans-Himalayas: Bashahar Kinnaur*, Delhi; -do- (2011) *Exploring Malana: An Ancient Culture Hidden In The Himalayas*, Delhi; -do- (2015) *Nathapanth in Western Himalaya*, Delhi; -do- (2015) *A Grammar of sTodpa -A Language of Lahul in the Western Himalaya, Delhi*; -do- (2015) *Nathapanth in Western Himalaya*, Delhi; -do- (2015) *Spiti: A Study in Socio-Cultural Traditions*, Delhi; -do- (2016) 'Chandra aur Bhaga ka Sangam aur Lahul ki sthapna', in *Shagun, Samarika, Layul Sursangam Society*, Dehli; -do- (2019 *The people of the upper valley : the Stodpas of Lahul in the Himalayas*, Delhi; -do- (2019) *Zong Gonpa of Village Tinno*, Delhi;-do- (2020) *Bhoti Parichay: Vyakaran aur Anuvad: Hindi Language*, Delhi; -do- (2020) *Stodpa Language of Lahul in the Himalaya*, Delhi; -do- (2020) *sTodpa Language of Lahul in the Himalaya*, Delhi; -do- (2021) *Ancient Lahul and Himalaya*, New Delhi.

Tobdan & C.Dorje,(1996) *Historical Documents from Western Trans-Himalaya, Lahul, Zanskar and Ladakh*, Delhi; -do- (2008) *Moravian Missionaries in Western Trans-Himalaya*, Delhi.

Tucci, Giuseppe,(1935) *The Temples of Western Tibet and Their Artistic Symbolism, Tsaparang*, III-2, New Delhi. English Translation: 1989; -do- (1971). *Travels of Tibetan Pilgrims in the Swat Valley*, Rome.

Vogel, J. Ph. (1902) ' Triloknath' in *Journal of the Asiatic Society of Bengal*, Vol. LXXI, Part I, Calcutta,(pp.35-40); -do- (1911) *Antiquities of Chamba*

State, Part I, Archaeological Survey of India, New Delhi, reprinted 1994.

Widorn, Verena & Gerald Kozicz. (2012). 'The Temple of Triloknath — A Buddhist Nagara Temple in Lahul', in *South Asian Studies*, 28:1, pp. 15-35.

Widorn, Verena (2008) 'Buddha Sakyamuni, Johling (Kyelong), Lahaul and Spiti,' in *Vision of an Enlightend King, A Centenial Bouquet of Himalayan Art from Bhuri Singh Museum Collection*, ed. Vijay Sharma (Chamba,Bhuri Singh Museum), pp.52-53; -do- (2020), 'From Padmasambhava to Go Tsangpa: Rethinking Religious Patronage in the Indian Himalayas between the 8th and 13th Centuries' in *Buddhism in Central Asia*, pp.151-188; -do- (2015) 'Traversing the Land of Siddhas and Dākinīs—Art Historical Evidences along the Buddhist Pilgrimage Routes through Lahul', in *Cultural Flows across the Western Himalaya*, ed. Patrick McAllister and others, Vienna, pp.189-235.

Widorn, V. & Michaela Kinberger (2009) 'Mapping the sacred landscape of Lahaul — The Karzha Khandroling mandala' in William Cartwright, Georg Gartner & Antje Lehn, eds. *Cartography and art: lecture notes in geoinformation and cartography*. Berlin: Springer-Verlag, pp. 292-304.

Index